Air Words

WRITING FOR BROADCAST NEWS

THIRD EDITION

JOHN HEWITT
San Francisco State University

Boston   Burr Ridge, IL   Dubuque, IA   Madison, WI   New York   San Francisco   St. Louis
Bangkok   Bogotá   Caracas   Kuala Lumpur   Lisbon   London   Madrid   Mexico City
Milan   Montreal   New Delhi   Santiago   Seoul   Singapore   Sydney   Taipei   Toronto

McGraw-Hill Higher Education

A Division of The McGraw-Hill Companies

Copyright © 2002 by The McGraw-Hill Companies, Inc. All rights reserved. Printed in the United States of America. Except as permitted under the United States Copyright Act of 1976, no part of this publication may be reproduced or distributed in any form or by any means, or stored in a database or retrieval system, without the prior written permission of the publisher.

6 7 8 9 0 QPD/QPD 0 9 8

Library of Congress Cataloging-in-Publication Data

Hewitt, John
    Air words : writing for broadcast news / John Hewitt—3rd ed.
      p. cm.
    Includes bibliographical references and index.
    ISBN 0-7674-2714-9
    1. Television broadcasting of news. 2. Broadcast journalism—Authorship.
I. Title.

    PN4784 T4 H48 2001
    808′.06607—dc21

                              2001026609

Sponsoring editor, Holly J. Allen; *production editor,* Jennifer Mills; *manuscript editor,* Ben Shriver; *design manager,* Susan Breitbard; *art manager,* Rennie Evans; *cover designer,* Joan Greenfield; *manufacturing manager,* Randy Hurst. This text was set in 9.5/13 Stone Serif by *in pages* and printed on 50# Champion Offset by Quebecor Printing Book Group.

This book is printed on acid-free paper.

www.mhhe.com

Contents

3 The Shift From Print to Effective Broadcast Copy   40

4   Writing the Compelling Lead   75

11　Television: Packages and Live Shots　173

12　Producing for All Media: Developing Stories　190

13 Creating Effective Newscasts   200

Preface

A lot has happened in the six years since the second edition of *Air Words*. We've moved into a new century without the world falling down. The 24-hour local cable news stations have survived the shakeout. News writers are struggling with the new deadlines that computerized newsrooms demand. The Internet has vaulted into the spotlight as a research and distribution medium, and major news corporations, merging furiously, have hired staffs to service the needs of the Internet news junkie. Internet radio is no longer just another way of reaching an audience but has its own unique stations that do not appear anywhere else. A lot of primary research and fact-checking is conducted on the Internet. I hope this new edition of *Air Words* will recognize these changes and provide a step toward this rapidly evolving world of the Internet.

Still, it's true that every news assignment reaches a moment when a reporter or writer must sit down at a keyboard and compose the story. The task is to sift through information, decide what to include and what to leave out, come up with a clever lead, infuse some perspective, fit the story into the producer's requested time frame, and in the case of broadcast or Internet radio, write for the spoken word.

For the student, this workbook is ready to help you with skills you will need in the world of spoken news. In these pages you will find a collection of definitions, rules, warnings, shortcuts, models, and exercises to sharpen your ability to write for spoken news. If you are currently working in newspapers or magazines, broadcast requires changes. You will be writing in the sometimes awkward world of speech patterns—awkward because they look different on the page. You will be working with interviews, sounds, and pictures recorded in the field—elements that force changes in the story design. The basic need to pass along timely reports of current events is still there, but the way of doing it is changed.

Also, you will find that style standards for the copy (such as using upper or lowercase, hyphenating numbers or not) vary from station to station, or market to market. That's fine. It's hard to get broadcast newspeople to agree on anything, including definitions. What this book defines as a package—a narrated television field report—is also called a takeout, an insert, a wraparound, or a field piece in different newsrooms. You might end up using a different term, whatever your instructor or news director suggests. At least you'll be able to say "Oh, they called that a *wrap* in the last place I worked."

In *Air Words* you will find hints, suggestions, and rules. These are not absolute. When you read "Use active voice! Put attribution first! Look out for pronouns!", think of these rules as recommendations toward a better broadcast style. They will help, but sometimes they can be ignored to add variety.

Finally, *Air Words* is one of the few writing texts to provide extensive drill and exercise for each fundamental style module. Whether it's ethics, writing in active voice, or placing soundbites in stories, each has built-in exercises to allow for growth in those areas. These modules have been retained to allow instructors to proceed at an individual pace in drilling students. At the same time, this format recognizes that instructors have strong theories about news gathering and story design—theories that come from years of experience. For that reason, many areas in the third edition still invite personalized curricular innovation, especially in the areas of story selection and producing. I hope the third edition achieves this goal: to stay grounded in the useful style and structure exercises while moving cautiously into the Internet age and news role changes of this new century.

So welcome to the world of writing for your co-worker's lips and the audience's ears. Work hard and you'll get the hang of voice-delivered news. Good luck.

ACKNOWLEDGMENTS

This book began as a series of handouts in broadcast news classes. It has gone through numerous revisions, and I appreciate all of the frank, useful, and often direct criticism from students in the Broadcast and Electronic Communication Arts Department at San Francisco State University.

Along the way, a number of people read all or part of the manuscript and offered help or encouragement, including Bill Rukeyser, then a newswriter at a television station in San Francisco; my colleagues at San Francisco State: Rick Houlberg, Ann Marshall, Art France, and Herb Kaplan; and the reviewers of this third edition: Rose Kundanis, Keene State College, and Jim Sequin, Robert Morris College.

My wife, Annette Blanchard, was always there with support and understanding. I also appreciate the work of my Mayfield/McGraw-Hill editor Holly Allen, production editor Jen Mills, and manuscript editor Ben Shriver.

Thanks to all. I couldn't have done it without you.

This book is dedicated to four former colleagues who were splendid thinkers and outstanding educators: Bill Wente, Buzz Anderson, and Herb Kaplan at San Francisco State University, and Jules Dundes at Stanford University. All are gone, but all had a wonderful dedication to teaching and to their students.

1

Radio, Television, and the Webcast

CHAPTER PREVIEW

This chapter covers the relationship between journalism and broadcast—whether it be over the air or the Internet. You'll learn why you must consider the special strengths of broadcast—the power of immediacy, voice recordings and visuals, emotion, and personal delivery. You'll examine research methods for assessing both community and Internet resources. You'll explore ethical questions involving broadcast news work. You'll find out the extra skills a journalist needs to become proficient in broadcast news.

GLOSSARY

ACTUALITY The term for audio or video field recordings of interviews or events. Portions may be used in a newscast.

ADVANCING THE STORY Updating, expanding, or re-sourcing the story to provide new and more accurate reporting.

BITE A portion of a recorded interview that is scheduled for use in a broadcast news story.

ETHICS The study of moral decision making in personal or social situations. Codes of ethics are frameworks and references for making decisions in news work.

PRIMARY SOURCE A story source who is either an eyewitness, someone affected by the events of the story, or an acknowledged expert on the situation.

PRONOUNCER The phonetic spelling of a word in a broadcast story. Usually the pronouncer is broken into syllables and placed in the copy behind the true spelling of the word. For example "King Abu Saud (SAH-AH-`UDE)." The pronouncer is the writer's responsibility.

SECONDARY SOURCE Person with information that is obtained from another who is a primary source. In this case, almost all news reporting would be considered a secondary source.

SOT   Short for sound on tape or disk. This alerts anyone working on the newscast that the audio portion will come from a recording.

SOUNDBITE   A portion of an actuality interview chosen for a story.

STREAMING VIDEO   The video portion of an Internet story. The quality depends upon the speed of the communication line.

TEMPLATE   The screen format of a news computer system. The template provides a place for information and newswriting.

WIRE CAPTURE   The ability of a news computer system to record, store, and display wire service stories when needed for data.

THIS BUSINESS OF NEWS

This workbook is about news stories and how to put them together. In its most simple definition, news is a timely report of changing current events. It's also supposed to be thoughtful, accurate, balanced, filled with perspective, and, when the occasion calls for it, cleverly done.

News reporters and writers prepare news for presentation. It is hoped they enjoy sifting through the blizzard of incoming news stimuli, working under deadline, and serving as a public striver for truth. All that aside, they should also delight in daily opportunities to craft their stories.

Much of what is studied as journalism concerns newspapers. Print journalism's writing style, reporting needs, story lengths, conventions, values, industry practices, and story variety are the venerated guideposts of this business.

Broadcast, on the other hand, is new. Misunderstood by many who believe it should act like a newspaper, broadcast has its own reporting needs, industry practices, writing styles, and story variety. In broadcast, you must write for speech patterns, design stories around the various sound and visual recordings made in the field, and work within severe time limitations. More than with a newspaper, the audience's needs must be considered.

WHAT AUDIENCE RESEARCH TELLS US

The general public consistently tells survey takers that radio, television, and the Internet are very important sources of news. The audience listens to radio, watches television, or logs onto the Internet not only for the latest and most immediate information but also because they can see and hear the people involved in the news and because they trust in the personal delivery of newscasters.

Listeners and viewers have an on-again, off-again relationship with newscasts. Researchers[1] have found that most of the radio audience and more than half of the television audience are doing something else while these newscasts are on the air. For the most part, over-the-air radio listeners are traveling in the car, while Internet radio and television listeners and viewers are at home cooking, eating dinner, taking care of children, lying in bed, or even reading newspapers. The Internet radio audience could be multitasking, so while your broadcast is on, they are viewing screens or finishing other tasks. With audience attention drifting in and out, it takes clever leads and a sharp broadcast style to bring them into each and every story.

Another problem—the audience gets one and only one chance to hear the story. Research has sorted out what the viewer or listener perceives, retains, and understands from the newscast.[2] Stories written in direct speech patterns, with the least complex phrasing, are the easiest to digest in that crucial single pass. Newswriters must work to develop a simple style that promotes the maximum understanding. Television writers also have to be aware that powerful visuals distract viewers and lessen comprehension.

BROADCAST'S STRENGTHS

We're all familiar with the advantages of newspapers. Newspapers can be read at any time, are portable, report massive amounts of news, have specialized sections, and—best of all—allow us to scan the pages and read only what we want. There is no question that many journalism practices are aimed at highlighting those qualities.

But broadcast has its own strengths: immediacy, field recordings, emotion, and personal delivery. These advantages guide decisions about what to stress in broadcast stories.

Strength 1: Immediacy

News is a collection of timely summaries of current events. People turn first to over-the-air or Internet radio and then to television for the latest information, the update, or the last review of the evening.[3] Internet coverage in terms of radio or streaming video television feeds is controversial—and was restricted in the 2000 Olympics because no one knew then how the new media's immediacy would affect the size of the audience loyal to the delayed television and radio reports.

Part of broadcast news work is a constant search for the update, the new information or angle that "advances" the story. To get this immediacy some radio news staffs never leave the office and, instead, do all reporting and interviews on the phone. In this way new leads can be prepared quickly. Television needs the pictures and spends huge sums on microwaves, uplink trucks, and satellites designed to link any location with their studio.

But this pursuit of immediacy can also be a drawback. While providing the audience with a chance to listen and watch as the action happens on breaking stories, television and radio staffs work under deadlines that compress time needed to evaluate sources and review information. If facts are not thoroughly checked, rumor can be put on the air.

There is also deserved criticism of the television live shot. Too often stations send reporters to the news location either with little information or else hours after the event is over. In many cases, the reporter would have had a chance to check facts and prepare a better story by staying in the newsroom. These are management decisions that often have little to do with news.

Strength 2: Field Recordings

Field recordings offer vivid actualities, soundbites, and visuals. Using these on the air gives the audience a chance to be on the scene of the event in progress. Radio or Internet radio has the rich natural sound of voices or happenings; television adds the visual dimension. When in the field, don't forget how valuable the audio and videotape will be for the story. Remember, audiences tell poll takers that one reason they watch television is they like to see and hear people in the news, so they can judge for themselves whether a person is telling the truth.

Strength 3: Emotion

For years print-based accounts reduced the visibility of emotion's role in events, concentrating instead on rational cause and effect or lists of details and names. Now broadcast actualities, soundbites, and visuals have restored emotion to an important place in stories.

But emotion is a tricky story angle to handle and must be kept in proper perspective. When pictures and actualities with strong emotion become a story's driving force, it rightfully raises charges of sensationalism. The goal is to uncover genuine sentiment and let it reveal itself. Emotion should be treated with great care.

Strength 4: Personal Delivery

How the reporter or anchor delivers the story is crucial to the audience's understanding. An effective newscaster needs a well-written script, a comfortable voice, and good pronunciation to communicate the item.

When the newscaster reads a story, it is as if the writer is speaking. As that writer, you must take great pains to write for conversational flow. This means smoothing the sentence flow, providing pronouncers (the pronunciation guides), checking the accuracy of the story, and preparing the actualities and visuals. Awkward, print-style writing in a broadcast script will make your entire news department look incompetent.

The personal-delivery advantage of broadcast creates an awkward situation for those who abuse it, however. Too much emphasis on personal delivery causes the newscast to cross the line into entertainment.

DIFFERENT STRENGTHS LEAD TO DIFFERENT APPROACHES

Radio and television reporters often use different methods from those used by print reporters to gather information about current events. Because the circulation of newspapers is limited by distance, the print medium tends to concentrate reporting in nearby cities. But the broadcast signal is easily beamed to a wider area, giving even tiny two-person radio news staffs a metropolitan area to cover. Therefore, broadcast staffs are structured differently.

- More research is done from the newsroom, and far fewer reporters are on the street.

- Concentration is on extensive coverage of a few important stories, rather than specialized beat reporting.
- Emphasis is on quick reactions to tips and information from many sources, including other news agencies.
- More staff positions go to engineers or photographers, whose job is to get recorded interviews and visuals.

When a news story is prepared, broadcast's strengths will often suggest a unique lead. On occasion, the lead might stress what's in the actualities or soundbites. Other times, it will highlight the story's immediacy or the newscaster's presentation ability. In any case, it is important to be aware that broadcast can choose its own angle for the story lead in accord with what's best for the medium and for the audience.

THE DIFFERENT LOOK OF BROADCAST

Broadcast stories are not only gathered in an unusual manner, they are designed to be scan-read in the newscast. They must mimic conversational English. Their sentence construction is shorter, more abrupt, and is built around phrasing. Although the period stays at the end of the sentence, many shops use special punctuation models, such as three dots to replace a comma. Here are examples of both print and broadcast.

UFO fans headed to big meet

Perris, CA.
Throngs of UFO fanatics are expected to meet sometime next week in the nation's capital to petition the federal government for the transcripts of UFO investigations in the '60s, according to Perry Outthere, the coordinator for the Southern California UFO Adherents society.

PAGE TAL SLUG   VIDEO   APPROVAL WRITER TRT

ORIGINATED:_____   MODIFIED _____   STATUS _____

U-F-O FANS ARE STAGING A MEETING IN THE NATION'S CAPITAL.
THEY WANT THE GOVERNMENT TO OPEN UP FILES. . .FILES THEY SAY CONTAIN INFORMATION ABOUT U-F-O SIGHTINGS.
ONE OFFICIAL OF THE U-F-O...

FIGURE 1.1
Left, *example of how a story would appear in print;* right, *how it would appear in broadcast.*

Notice that the differences are not just stylistic but structural, too. The broadcast story is a narrative and, using shorter sentences, releases facts a little at a time. It is written for the ear.

In almost every exercise that follows in this workbook, we'll be encouraging you to write to mimic speech patterns. Before you do, you should see what your speech looks like. Try this next exercise.

((• EXERCISE 1-A •))

What Your Speech Looks Like

For this exercise, you'll need an audio recorder and a word processor. The purpose of this exercise is to produce a printed version of your normal speech patterns.

To begin, read the following situation several times. Then put down the book, and using the recorder, record your account of the story as you understand it and as if you were telling it to a friend. This is meant to be impromptu, even casual. Don't write what you are going to say. This narrative should run about :45 (45 seconds).

When you finish, type an exact transcription of what you said. Be truthful. The transcript should include every stumble, half-sentence, "uhmm," "awesome," "like," or whatever you said to describe what was going on.

Situation

The location: The city's Leopard Creek Zoo.
The event: Two great pandas arrive amidst a flurry of civic activity. The mayor, the delegation from China, and a lot of zookeepers, onlookers, reporters, and television cameras are here also. A large delivery truck pulls up, and after several speeches, the pandas are taken from a large flatbed trailer in special wooden packing cases. The pandas are on loan for two months and will live in a special climate-controlled building that the zoo has for animals with special needs. Zookeepers will be feeding the pandas blue bamboo shoots, the only food the creatures will eat. It'll be two weeks before the public is allowed to view them.

WHAT ARE SOME DRAWBACKS OF BROADCAST?

Earlier in this chapter we discussed structural problems that occur with overemphasis on the broadcast strengths. Too much immediacy and you lose your ability to evaluate and edit the information. Too much emotional content and you begin to slide into sensationalism. Too much emphasis on personal delivery and you edge toward entertainment (infotainment).

Other drawbacks have to do with the way newsrooms operate. One critical drawback is the inflexibility of formats for stories. At some commercial television stations, read-only stories are limited to :30, stories with a simple soundbite can go :45, and reporter packages are allowed a full minute. At some fast-moving commercial all-news radio stations, those format times might be half as long: a reader might be limited to :15. These time constraints are meant to produce a fast-moving newscast, but limits like these often are shortsighted and hamper thoughtful journalism. Oddly enough, the year 2000 report of the Project for Excellence in Journalism at the Columbia University Graduate School of Journalism found that the stations which consistently have longer stories are the most successful ones.[4]

An industry drawback is competition. In even the smallest markets, there is usually a competitor for a radio or television news operation; in the big markets, there can be many news crews out covering the same story. This head-banging competition, once the norm in newspapers, can be all-consuming when breaking stories must be covered. Staffs are often told they must get it first to be "number one" in their market. The old adage "Get it right! Then get it first!" still applies.

Also, commercial broadcasting exists in an industry that is not news-based but performance-based. Your immediate news manager, the news director, may or may not have been a journalist. The person to whom the news director reports probably did not rise up through the news ranks. So news decisions often become accounting or sales decisions, and decisions on ethical questions might be made by someone who has no appreciation of journalism. That can cause morale problems.

RESEARCH METHODS

Research for this business occurs on a deadline and usually involves searching primary printed sources, studying old clips, or talking to people who are very leery of what you do. Journalists should be cautious of single-source stories. It is significant that the Project for Excellence in Journalism at Columbia used (a) multiple sources and (b) expertise of sources as two of its checkpoints for assessing quality in broadcast news. There is a solid benefit in talking to multiple primary sources. This is often the way to find multiple viewpoints, new story ideas, follow-up ideas, and confirming facts. In this millennium, no journalists worth their salt will ever succeed without mastering at least two important tools: the telephone and the Internet.

Telephone Research for Local Information

One old-time news reporter had a rule: Never get off the phone until you have the information you called for. Talking to sources is still the best way to get local information. Here are some useful tips:

- Get a headset if you are comfortable with that.
- Be prepared to write down information in readable notes.
- Get as many directories as you can. Locate sources on the Internet, such as company phone and contact lists. Make your own list of beat calls, to be done if you have the time.

Sources can be divided into two camps: primary and secondary. To identify primary sources, ask the same questions that might be asked in court. Is this person an expert? Can this person be expected to offer an unbiased opinion about the story? Is this person an eyewitness to the action? Finally, is this person directly affected by the action and free to talk about it?

If they don't have strong credentials for expert testimony, or if they are merely retelling the eyewitness story they heard from someone else, or if they just knew someone affected by the story, then people qualify only as secondary sources.

Internet Research

A decade ago this was only a dream, but now a journalist can't live without the Internet. You don't have to be an investigative pit bull to use the Internet for research. Search engines, all-encompassing databases, maps, and phone directories are a delight for those who know how to use them. But research opportunities in this area change constantly, and today's hot search engine may not exist tomorrow. The following sections offer some exercises you can undertake to make the Internet and Web work for you.

While the consolidation of Internet operations allows for very sophisticated searching, some simpler, clearly identifiable tasks that the Internet does nicely are described in the next sections.

Searching Reference Works and Archives You should be able to tap into traditional reference works and local news archives for background on current events or places. Often, this is a trial and error search. In many cities, local newspapers allow online access to current editions, as well as archival search possibilities. A substantial number of national news agencies, both print and broadcast, offer access to news information. Some, though, like the *New York Times,* charge for archival access.

(((EXERCISE 1-B)))

Looking for Archives

Using local Internet resources as outlined by your instructor, find at least three recent stories about each of these topics:

1. the local crime rate

2. a local environmental battle between developers and citizens

3. local business activity, cast in either a good or a bad light

Accessing Databases You should be able to access central database lists maintained by libraries and universities. Accessing local university and library reference desks is a matter of locating the institution and continuing the search until you get into their databases. Most university libraries are up-to-date with online search assistance, proprietary databases, and access to consortium-agreement depositories at other institutions. You also might access the individual databases' search information screens to pick up tips particular to that database. At San Francisco State University, you can choose to search only the campus archives or be automatically linked to resources from other California libraries. By doing the latter, you can access the California Digital Library, which includes the holdings of the California State Library, the largest government depository in the state.

(((EXERCISE 1-C)))

Looking for Library Assistance

Using local Internet resources as outlined by your instructor, find out which databases exist at your local college or municipal library and how to gain access to them.

Using Hot Search Engines   You should be able to search competently on whatever search engine is the current hot one. Search engines are very user friendly, but a quick grasp of specialized search techniques allows you to conduct a search that doesn't result in 300,000 possible sites. Many search engines use standardized search request protocols.

- To limit searches, use the particular search parameters of the individual search engine.
- If you put a "+" before a word, it generally means you want the exact same word in the found location.
- If you put "and" between two words in the search, the engine will look only for sites with both words.
- If you put quotation marks around two words, it will search only for sites that have those two words in that order.
- For some searches, you can use up to 150 qualifying words to limit the search.

((‹ **EXERCISE 1-D** ›))

General Searches

Using a major search engine, search for:

1. a site that provides information about government Superfund toxic site cleanup
2. a site offering information on safety defects in light pickup trucks
3. a group arguing against the proliferation of land mines in the world

---

Retrieving Government Data   You should be able to access government reports, documents, and databases for local area, state, regional, and national governments. For instance, in the San Francisco area, you can search local to national sites:

- *San Francisco Cityspan* (http://www.ci.sf.ca.us/) for city records
- *San Francisco NeighborNet* (http://www.neighbornet.org/) for local organizations, news events, community resources, volunteer opportunities, local police information, and links to the media

- *Association of Bay Area Governments* (ABAG) (http://www.abag.org/home.html) for regional governmental planning material

- *State of California Home Page* (http://www.ca.gov/s/govt/) for elected officials, courts, government services and agencies, elections, laws, codes, and regulations

- *Google.com Regional Directory* (http://www.google.com/Top/Regional/), an Internet search service to find a gateway to locate a government agency or online publication

- *GPO Access: Finding Aids* (http://www.access.gpo.gov/su_docs/tools.html), the U.S. government gateway to online federal resources

- *INFOMINE* (http://infomine.ucr.edu/search/govpubsearch.phtml), a search site providing keyword, title, and subject searches for government Web sites

Each city, area, and state will have different access sites for local government documents. These are particularly useful in expanding or backgrounding public policy stories.

(((**EXERCISE 1-E**)))

Finding Government Sites

Find three sites that tell you about airliner safety.
Find three sites that tell you about regional government planning.
Get the phone numbers and bios of your local congressional representatives.

Locating Individuals   You should be able to locate an expert or track down an individual and find a way to contact that person either by e-mail or telephone. This type of search is getting more user friendly. Telephone white pages are available online through MSN, Lycos, and Yahoo! Type in a name, and the search program will provide a list of phone numbers and addresses. Type in a business, and it'll find yellow page listings. Type in a phone number, and it will tell you who owns it.

How do you find an expert? Use business directories to locate the firm that you want, and then using their Web sites, or simple phone calls, proceed from there.

Finding the Expert

Using the Internet, locate the name and phone number of an expert on:

1. auto braking systems

2. jail reform programs

3. elementary education programs

ETHICS INVOLVING NEWS WORK AND BROADCAST

What does it mean when we hear that journalists have low ethical standards? For most critics, it is a way of implying that journalists will do anything—illegal, immoral, or whatever—to get a story. Journalists, they say, will opt for the greatest greed over the greatest good and are only interested in building circulation or ratings. Are they right? I hope not.

The study of ethics is the study of decision making when a decision might lead to good or bad results. Ethical choices confront news staffs on a daily basis, whether they concern news-gathering methods, information release, or story choice.

Journalists are usually involved in two areas of consequences: personal and societal. In the area of personal ethical decisions, the difficulties lie in the protection of confidential sources, distortion of news items, outright lies, self-censorship, and taking gifts for news items. In the societal professional area there are issues of legal reporting, defamation and slander, checkbook journalism or buying information, cronyism with news sources, misrepresentation, invasion of privacy, use of stolen documents, and sensationalism.

That's a big list and a dangerous one. Journalists work in the community and use the public trust as a shield for their work. Because they seldom have any legal standing beyond that of a private citizen, and because the First Amendment does not protect the news-gathering area, reporters are often at odds with other rights and privileges when gathering information. Even so-called shield laws, designed to protect unpublished notes and important sources, seldom stand up to judicial challenges when pitted against the right to a fair trial.

Providing a checklist so journalists can test their decisions is a difficult task; there are too many variables in every case study to claim any one as a model. Instead, writers of ethics books have tried to set up general guidelines for decisions.

Louis Day, in his book *Ethics in Media Communications: Cases and Controversies,* lists a simple progression of six categories a journalist should consider when facing a particularly troubling situation. These are:

A. individual conscience (your own moral standards)

B. objects of moral judgment (who is affected by your story)

C. financial supporters (the company you work for)

D. the institution (journalism itself)

E. professional colleagues (your co-workers)

F. society (general taboos against certain actions)

As you can see, consideration begins with the individual's own moral conscience, then considers those immediately affected, before considering larger and more inclusive groups. In examining the situation in which a journalist is asked to reveal the identity of a confidential source during a petty burglary trial, the decision process might go this way:

First, define the problem. Be careful to consider all possible outcomes and individuals and groups affected—a court is asking the journalist to reveal a source's name; the journalist has promised complete confidentiality; if the journalist refuses, the judge is ready to send the journalist to jail. Next, consider each of the six categories.

In the area of individual conscience (category A), the journalist may decide that her own personal standards and values will be harmed. On the flip side, the jail option and ensuing court appearances may be damaging to the journalist's personal career and family.

Considering category B, the objects of moral judgment, the question concerns the effect on the source and on the defendant in the trial. Would releasing the source's name put this person in danger? Would it cost the source his job? Would holding back the name injure the defendant's possibility for a fair trial? Is the name that important?

For category C, yes, it is necessary to consider the effect on the journalist's employer. Court sanctions and fines have put media companies out of business, and the continued fight against the judge's contempt power might cost the station thousands of dollars in fines and legal costs. Can the business stand the cost?

For category D, the institution, will this stand by the journalist be good for the credibility of journalism in general? Will the publicity damage the reputation of all journalists who work for the station and who work at similar jobs in other stations or in other media? Recall the national outrage over an NBC producer's decision to use model rocket motors to assist the ignition of spilled gasoline in the testing of a truck's fuel tank. A national poll by the Times Mirror company found that the network's credibility had fallen significantly in the public's eyes; management's concerns then possibly brought about the resignation of the NBC news president, as well as the dismissal of several staff members.

In the area of professional colleagues, category E, then, the journalist should consider if her co-workers would support the decision. In this case, withholding the name of a confidential source, the journalist might easily have them on her side because this has always been a journalist's badge of honor—not to reveal a source's name, even when threatened with jail.

The final area to question is category F, society. This is the area of social responsibility. Journalists should believe that a society is stronger when a source can contact a reporter without fear of retribution, and thus allow journalism to occupy the watchdog role. It might be a tougher decision if the case involved broadcast of overly violent sensational video. In that case, societal reaction would play a larger part in the decision.

(((**EXERCISE 1-G**)))

Ethical Analysis

Read the following situations, then define the problem and outline possible outcomes in the six areas of ethical consideration.

Situation 1

You are producer for a local television evening newscast. Your photographer returns to the station with video of a man who jumps from a downtown ledge in a suicide. Your news director thinks this is great actuality and should go in the newscast. What do you think? What must you take into account? Do you support or oppose using the video?

Situation 2

You are a radio reporter who returns from a news conference called by a local critic of the city's police chief. In speaking about the latest controversial incident, the critic, a politician who is obnoxious himself, becomes confused and actually issues a strong statement supporting the chief. You've been waiting a long time to get back at this politician. Is this the time to use the confused bite without perspective?

Situation 3

You are a television reporter covering a highly publicized corruption trial in your city. One of the defense lawyers slips you some sealed grand jury transcripts with new information about the case. Although the judge has made a specific statement forbidding any revelations from the transcripts during the trial, you believe that the information is in the public interest. What do you do, and what might be the consequences?

(continued)

(continued)

Situation 4

You are a reporter for a small radio station. The local gas and electric utility offers to fly you to the new hydroelectric plant for a story. They will provide transportation, lodging, and meals for two days in an attractive resort area while you do the story. Your station could never pay for this. Do you take the offer?

Situation 5

While reporting a story about an accident, you and your camera-person are asked by a nurse attending a severely injured person to transport him to the hospital. There is no other vehicle close by. Your station, however, needs the story for the next newscast. Should you stop reporting and assume the role of a concerned citizen?

Situation 6

Your station has received quite a nice buy of advertising time from a laser hair removal clinic. Then you find you have been assigned to do a feature on laser hair removal, and the assignment desk has sent you to this same clinic to shoot the story. Should you do the story or complain about being used?

Situation 7

A criminal in a sensational local case has never talked to the media. Now, she is calling you, asking if you'd like an exclusive personal interview. The catch is that she wants $300 to help her child get an operation. Your station can afford this. Do you take the interview?

Situation 8

Your reporter comes back with an interview of a very newsworthy person who has refused to talk to the media. You find out that the reporter wore a wireless mike and the photographer shot the interview from a van parked a half-block away. Should you use the tape? Does it matter whether or not this individual, who is involved in a public scandal, didn't know she was being taped?

WRITING ON NEWS COMPUTERS

Increasingly complex computer systems that run on local networks and servers are finally the norm for larger radio staffs and most television stations. The beauty of news computer systems such as Basys, NewsStar, AP, EZNews, or AVIDNews is their ability to do a multitude of jobs and eliminate paper shuffling and organizational busywork. Along with the ability to write and rewrite at will, the systems will capture, sort, and store wire copy; allow searches of archives and databases for keywords in copy; format, time, and direct the stories to the proper editors and newscasts; operate as a teleprompter when needed; work as electronic mail, memo, and file systems; allow field writing and sending of scripts; and provide the writer with a place to store individual stories.

The process of writing itself is easier on news computers. The newswriter can call up needed wire copy or internal information on the story, store pertinent parts

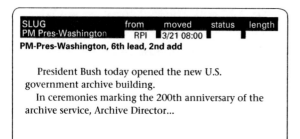

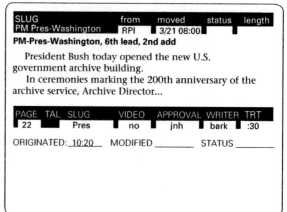

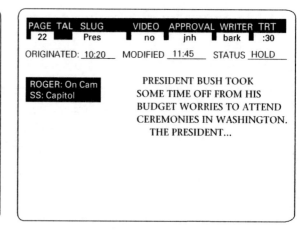

FIGURE 1.2

This is the process for computer systems. Top left, *the writer calls up the wire information and scrolls through it to find what is needed.* Top right, *splitting the screen, the writer fills in the needed template information, setting up story destination and other information.* Bottom left, *the writer then composes the story with the database on the screen.* Bottom right, *finally, the computer reformats the story into proper news script format, before sending the story to the printer for scripts and to the prompter.*

on a split screen, and write the story with the database on half-screen. Given the right prompts, the computer will format the story, place it in the newscast rundown, time the story, backtime the newscast, and print it in whatever format the anchors want.

There are, of course, disadvantages to news computer writing. Using broadcast-prepared wire copy as a source leads to copycat writing at the local level. The desire to change or innovate in the copy is removed, and often the stories will sound similar on many different stations.

CHAPTER SUMMARY

This chapter has covered news, reporters, the different strengths of newspaper and broadcast media, and the unique skills you must acquire, in addition to writing, for work in broadcast.

News is a collection of current events summaries, salted with perspective, culled from all that happened, and packaged for a particular medium. Broadcast's strengths are immediacy, field recordings, emotions, and personal delivery. The drawbacks are too little time, the tendency toward sensationalism and entertainment, and problems of the broadcast industry itself.

Novice radio news workers must be able to research a story, whether using conventional methods or Internet search skills. They must know how to contact an interviewee, get permission for recording, ask questions, record the interview, pull the best bite, write the story around it, and often read the news on the air. Everyone should have an ethical framework for evaluating news practices and stories. Increasingly complex news computer systems will mean staffs must train for these new skills and be versed in systems now available.

NOTES

1. For research on usage, see Doris Graber's book *Processing the News: How People Tame the Information Tide* (New York: Longman, 1984) or the article "The Attention Factor in Recalling Television News," *Journal of Communication* 33 (1983).

2. There are two good books on this topic. The first is Graber's, mentioned in Note 1, and the other is John Robinson and Mark Levy's, *The Main Source: Learning from Television News* (Beverly Hills, CA: Sage Publications, 1986).

3. There are many polls that arrive at this finding. The most quoted is the venerable Roper Poll, done in 1984 for the Television Information Office in New York. Although many new ones are around, this poll is repeatedly brought out for public discussion.

4. The report from the Project for Excellence in Journalism (for the year 2000) at the Graduate School of Journalism of Columbia University studied 49 stations in 15 cities. It found that stations at which 40 percent of the stories were one minute or longer actually were attracting audiences in 2000, but that stations where the stories were shorter often had falling ratings.

2

The Mechanics of the Script: Copyediting, Fact Checking, Research, and Defamation

CHAPTER PREVIEW

This chapter covers the basic elements of the broadcast script and the basic goals of broadcast journalism: accuracy, fairness, solid coverage, and clear presentation. It also examines how well-executed scripts can promote information retention, by using elements such as simplicity, detail exclusion, and rounding off. It includes a general discussion of basic libel/slander/invasion of privacy concerns.

GLOSSARY

BACKGROUNDER A story used to expand history and perspective on a current news event or situation.

CART The cartridge with the recording or actuality that will be inserted into a radio newscast.

CG Short for character generated. This refers to electronically produced numbers and letters that are placed on the screen, often over other video, to give names, details, or directions. Also known as a *key, lower third super, title, font,* and others.

DEFENSE Conditions in defamation law that either absolve or lessen the responsibility for libel/slander/invasion of privacy.

(end/end) or (# # #) In some newsrooms, marks that are placed at the end of the story to indicate there are no additional pages.

INCUE (also abbreviated as **I.C.**) A term sometimes written on scripts that use actualities or soundbites. The incue usually includes the first four words of the bite. That helps identify the right actuality and whether or not it is cued correctly.

INVASION OF PRIVACY A form of defamation that, when broadcast, is true but injurious. Definitions of invasion of privacy vary from state to state.

LIBEL A form of character defamation that, when broadcast, is false. The definitions of libel vary from state to state.

(more/more) In some newsrooms, a mark that is placed at the bottom of a script page to indicate the story continues on the next page. Its use is a matter of individual newsroom style.

_O/C A television script abbreviation for on-camera. This indicates to the director that the picture and sound come from the newscaster reading in the studio. *Live* is also used.

OUTCUE (also known as **endcue** and abbreviated as O.C. or E.C.) A phrase that usually includes the last four words of an actuality or soundbite. This helps the engineer, producer, or director know when to cue the newscaster to resume reading. Although the incue is often unnecessary, the outcue is vital on a script.

PRIVILEGED SITUATION In defamation law, any situation in which the court restricts libel charges because of the needs of reporting for public knowledge. These situations include true and accurate reports of courts and lawmaking bodies.

PROMPTER A system for placing the written news scripts on a flat glass plate in front of the studio camera. Usually, the computer handles this function, or on older systems paper scripts are taped together and run on a belt in front of a camera.

REAX (short for *reaction*) A type of follow-up story. Also, it is used as an abbreviation in many broadcast news situations.

REMOTE A story that originates in the field and is often broadcast directly from a field location. A remote is quite often live; however, to make this point, some stations refer to these as "live remotes."

RUNDOWN The story order for a newscast. Also called the *"stack,"* the *format,* or the *lineup.*

SLANDER A form of defamation that is generally spoken, but is injurious and false. Definitions of slander vary from state to state.

SIDEBAR A story that explores another angle of a major news story. It could be a backgrounder, a profile on one of the people involved, or an explanation of terms or complex procedures in the story.

SOT Short for sound on tape. This alerts anyone working on the newscast that the audio portion will come from videotape.

SLUG A single-word identifier for a news story. It is chosen when the story is assigned and should remain the same until the story is broadcast. It will also be applied to all parts of the story, and to carts in radio and videotape in television.

TRT Total running time. This refers to a tape's time from the beginning of the tape until the end. It is used for the tape only, not for written copy.

TST Total story time. This refers to a story's running time from beginning to end, usually including the TRT of the tape within the story. It is not used as commonly as TRT.

VO or VOICE OVER A television news story format that uses a studio newscaster for picture and audio but inserts videotape for visuals during a portion of the story.

BROADCAST SCRIPTS ARE DIFFERENT

Punctuation: Each Station Has Its Style

Broadcast news copy is written for the ear. It is designed to be spoken and to be heard. As such, it will mimic speech patterns and oral storytelling, rather than the prose display you see in newspapers or even in this workbook. Broadcast style is designed to make broadcast copy more readable. To do this, it uses visual punctuation, rather than the complete set of print-style marks.

From this point on, the news script examples in this book will use broadcast style punctuation. Although some stations use commas, our style replaces them with three dots (…) We also use a period (.) or a question mark (?) at the end of a sentence. No other marks are used. Quotation marks are omitted because they aren't meant to be read. If you add a segment that is a direct quote to a story, then you would write the word *quote* into the script. Emphasis is added not by quotation marks but by using some device in the newswriting computer system to highlight the word or by underlining it on the paper copy of the script.

Styling: UPPERCASE or Upper and Lowercase

Each individual newsroom has a style for writing. Some anchors hate all UPPER-CASE copy, while others demand it. Every station has its own method. For this book, however, we will use all uppercase examples simply to allow them to stand out from the workbook's informational copy. This does not endorse one system or the other.

The Story Slug

Producers or editors usually assign a single word identifier called a *slug* to each story. Its purpose is to standardize the identification of this story. The slug stays the same through the entire day, ending up as the listing on the newscast rundown. It's wise to use a single-word slug that relates to the topic. In a story about federal action on banking, you might use "BANK." Later, if that story grew wider during the day, you might use composite slugs, such as "BANK-FDIC" or "BANK-REAX" or "BANK-JOBS," to cluster all of the topics for this particular story. In most cases, the slug goes in the upper left-hand corner, along with your initials and a time indicator (usually the date or newscast); however, this is up to the individual newsroom style and varies widely. A slugline for this example would be BANK/jnh/6pm. In news computer systems, the slug is entered into the template information and the computer places the slug.

There is no industrywide standard for exactly which information goes into a slug. Follow your local newsroom style.

```
BANK/jnh/6pm


_____  O/C    PRESIDENT BUSH

                 TODAY IS DEFENDING

                 HIS...
```

FIGURE 2.1
*The slug is positioned at top left
of script. A computer system will
format it onto the script.*

TECHNICAL INFORMATION: PRODUCTION CUES

It is the writer's job in broadcast to provide the technical information for production cues to elements of the scripts. The terms used vary from station to station, depending on the size of the staff or the historical use of local styles. Technical terms also differ for radio and television.

Radio News Scripts

Because radio does not employ a large control room staff, the scripts do not need extensive technical information. Although printers now pound out the script pages, a radio script extends across the page with 1-inch margins. This gives a :04 line, so a :30 story would be about eight lines. Double space between lines, unless your newsroom requires triple-spaced intervals.

Technical information is usually a matter of indicating which cart or storage server you'll be using, whether or not it is cued, what the incue and the outcue are, and what the TRT is on the actuality. This is an example of a radio script:

BANK/jnh/6pm

    FEDERAL BANK EXAMINERS ARE SAYING

TODAY THEY WILL INVESTIGATE NEWTON

SAVINGS AND LOAN FOR CHARGES OF FRAUD.

    SOME DEPOSITORS SAY THEY ARE AFRAID

THEY'LL LOSE THEIR MONEY.

    (cart #1F TRT=:07)

    Incue: "We think this is a scandal..."

    Outcue: "...are prepared for anything."

(Verbatim: "We think this is a scandal that will

bring down this bank. We are prepared for

anything.")

    THE INVESTIGATION COULD BEGIN AS EARLY

AS TUESDAY.

Notice that each actuality includes a tape running time, or TRT, an incue and an outcue. Often, local style will require a verbatim transcript of the actuality or a précis summarizing the actuality.

Television News Scripts

Because both the production and news staffs are much larger in television, it is more crucial to have the accurate technical information on a script intended for a live newscast. To do this, the TV news page traditionally has been split in half, with the left side used for the instructions to the director and the right half for the material to be read, called the *copy block*. Most computer systems now automatically print all the left-side cues for the director; however, the writer must include the appropriate codes in the text copy block.

Instructions to the Director

For television, it is vital that the director's instructions be accurate and clear. But be aware that what you learn in this workbook may not be the same terminology you'll use at a certain station. Many stations use different terms for the production cues.

It is also important that the direction on the left side of the script matches the point in the copy where you want the change made. It is always advisable to make any switches at the beginning of sentences or phrases that begin a new copy line.

Always write your story first, and don't add any directions until you've come close to finishing a good copy. When that is done, add the slugline and the director's information. This includes:

- instructions about reading from the studio (O/C, or LIVE)
- when a graphic might be inserted (CG FULL)
- when the newscaster is reading over a videotape (VO)
- when the visual and audio come from a tape (SOT)
- when there is a live shot (REMOTE)
- whatever times you need (TRT or TST)
- whatever end-of-page mark is appropriate [(end/end), (# # #), or (more/more)]

Figure 2.2 provides an example of a television news script page.

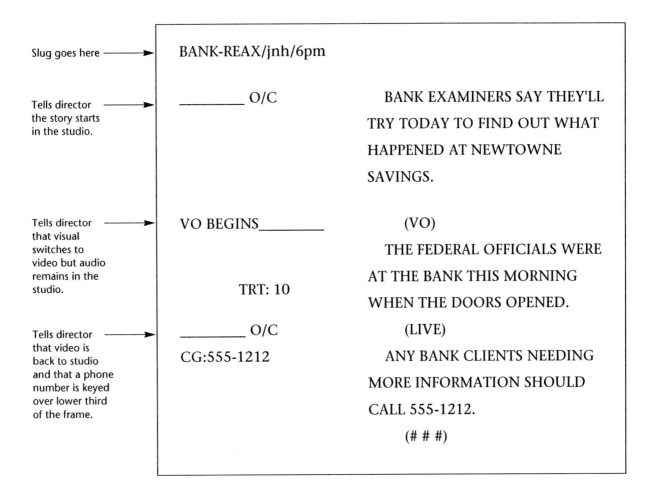

FIGURE 2.2
Television news copy with director's instructions.

READABLE COPY

Revising and marking scripts in broadcast is quite different from copyediting in print. In radio and TV, the idea is to produce copy that can be read quickly and clearly. It often doesn't matter what it looks like. To accomplish this, a broadcast editor uses heavy marks that totally hide unwanted words, and marks to indicate the flow across a gap. In broadcast, because you cannot read backwards, you cannot put in a transposition mark, such as

MOVIE HOLLYWOOD

Figure 2.3 gives an example of both unmarked and marked copy. The goal is to block out what is unwanted, and clearly write in what is needed. The reason for adding the particular marks it shows will be discussed in the next section.

MAYOR/jnh/6pm	MAYOR/jnh/6pm

_____ O/C THE MAYOR
ANNOUNCED AT A
NEWS
CONFERENCE
TODAY THAT THE
CITY WILL
SPONSOR AN
URBAN FAIR.
  SHE SAYS THAT
THE FAIR WILL
COST 23.45
MILLION
DOLLARS.
  IT WILL BE
LOCATED IN THE
FORT WILLIAMS
MALL PARKING
LOT AND SHOULD
RUN TWO
WEEKENDS IN
AUGUST.
    (# # #)
	_____ O/C THE MAYOR
	~~ANNOUNCED AT A~~
	~~NEWS~~ *Says*
	~~CONFERENCE~~
	~~TODAY THAT~~ THE
	CITY WILL
	SPONSOR AN
	URBAN FAIR.
	  SHE SAYS THAT
	THE FAIR WILL
	COST ~~23.45~~ *nearly 23*
	MILLION
	DOLLARS.
	  IT WILL BE
	LOCATED IN THE
	FORT WILLIAMS
	MALL PARKING
	LOT AND SHOULD
	RUN TWO
	WEEKENDS IN
	AUGUST.
	    (# # #)

FIGURE 2.3
The copy on the left needs editing. On the right, the marked copy is ready to be read on the air.

READABILITY

It's not just the marks on the page, but the basic sentence flow and amount of detail that makes a story readable. Here are some structural elements that help readability.

Sentence Length

A long sentence may work if it has comfortable breathing pauses and a simple topic. But that's the exception, and you'll want to be on the lookout for long, complex sentences, anything over three seconds. Try breaking the longer ones into two sentences, each of perhaps 11 to 15 words or fewer. This is not a hard and fast rule but only a guideline.

Contractions

These are usable in broadcast. You don't have to shy away from *wasn't, she'll, isn't,* or *it's.* They are more conversational. Use them.

Detail Exclusion

This is one time when story design considers the listener or viewer's needs. There is no definitive information about how many facts a listener can remember; however, studies show that a few facts presented in the least complex sentences have the best chance of staying with the audience. Review the information and decide what must get into the story and what will confuse it. You are looking for the most significant fact or facts. Some suggestions for items to exclude:

- *Middle initials.* These are unnecessary unless the individual demands that they be included or there is a historical reason to include them, such as adding the initial to President George W. Bush's name to distinguish him from his father.

- *Ages.* In most cases, these are unimportant. Obviously, if a 97-year-old man robs a store, you've got a different angle to the story. But if the robber was 34 years old, there is nothing newsworthy in that.

- *Addresses.* Newspapers routinely put these in; broadcasters routinely ignore them.

- *Decimal places.* Any figure with decimal places has little chance of being remembered. Count those out almost immediately unless you are convinced they are vital to the story. Round off.

- *Unnecessary geographical data.* Don't bore your audience with streets and areas you know. Evaluate whether it is useful to say the story happened in the Wilson Heights District.

- *Unnecessary attribution.* Decide whether it's necessary to give the source's name.

- *Unnecessary full titles.* Either eliminate or shorten most titles. An "under-secretary for Middle Eastern and Indian Subcontinental Affairs" could become a "State Department official."

Here's an example of copy with too much detail:

HOLIDAY PAGEANT ORGANIZERS ARE NOW SAYING THIS YEAR'S PARADE WILL BE THE BEST EVER.
THE VICE PRESIDENT FOR PARADE OPERATIONS AND LOGISTICS CAROLINE B. FOGLESON SAYS THERE WILL BE 20 FLOATS OVER THE COURSE OF 97 MINUTES AND 30 SECONDS...AND THAT COMES TO A FLOAT PASSING BY EVERY TWO-POINT-THREE MINUTES.
FOGLESON SAID THE PARADE WILL LEAVE THE TENTH STREET HOLDING CENTER AT 9 A-M...AND THEN WIND ITS WAY DOWN BRAXTON STREET BEFORE FINISHING UP AT THE TOWN SQUARE.

Numbers as Spoken Copy

When writing numbers to be read, there are some helpful rules:

- Some suggest hyphens to connect all parts of the number and the nouns that are modified. This depends on the individual newsroom style.

  23-COWS

  465-DAYS

- Spell out numbers from 1–11. Spell out decimal qualifiers (e.g., million, thousand, point)

  ONE-COW

  FOUR-THOUSAND-DAYS

- Except for dates, never use four digits in one number. For example, 999 is okay, but 1,999 must be written out.

  ONE-THOUSAND-999

  ONE-MILLION-990-THOUSAND-AND-FOUR-SHRIMP

  ONE-THOUSAND-FOUR-DOLLARS-AND-12-CENTS.

- Never use the $ for money. Always spell out *dollars.*

  26-DOLLARS

  46-THOUSAND-DOLLARS

  A THREE-MILLION-DOLLAR-PLANT

- Spell out any qualifying symbols that may be misread (e.g., %)

  26-PERCENT

  13-DEGREES

Rounding Off

Broadcast newswriters often face stories that contain large amounts of data—percentages, numbers, dollar amounts, and so on. If your goal is to inform the audience in one reading of the story, then you should practice rounding off some of these details.

If your story includes the number $24,473.25 as a city budget figure, you can round it off to "almost 25-thousand-dollars." While it is not the most accurate figure, it is close enough to give the audience an approximation of the amount. When appropriate, change something like 9.56% into "almost ten percent" or "nearly one-tenth." For print journalists, rounding off is unnecessary. For broadcast, it gives your audience a chance to remember the information.

Here's an example to work on.

(((**EXERCISE 2-A**)))

What Needs To Be Rounded Off?

Rewrite this copy, rounding off the data for broadcast.

BUDGET/jnh/6pm

THE MAR VISTA ESTATES CITY COUNCIL IS MAKING PUBLIC ITS BUDGET FIGURES FOR NEXT YEAR.

THE POLICE DEPARTMENT HAS ASKED FOR $234,344...THE FIRE DEPARTMENT NEEDS $121,323...THAT'S UP BY 21.2 PERCENT...AND THE CITY LIBRARY REQUESTED $86,721.

THESE AMOUNTS SHOW AN AVERAGE INCREASE OF 17.24 PERCENT FOR ALL DEPARTMENTS.

Details

Review this story and copyedit or rewrite it on another page.

PLANT/jnh/2pm

THE $24,630,243 SEWAGE TREATMENT TERTIARY REFINEMENT FACILITY...WHICH IS LOCATED ON THE SHORE-LINE AT BREMEMERS COVE...WILL BE PUT IN AN OPERATIONALLY SUSPENDED SITUATION NEXT WEEK.

SEWAGE ADMINISTRATOR B. MELFORD SAYS THEY ARE DOING THIS BECAUSE OF THE FACT THAT A CONDITION EXISTS THAT ALLOWS UNPROCESSED AND UNTREATED WASTE EFFLUENT TO INTERMINGLE WITH RIVER WATER DURING HEAVY RAINS IN THE WINTER MONTHS.

A 14-DAY MAINTENANCE LOOP WILL FOLLOW THE SHUTDOWN.

BEFORE YOU WRITE

Review Newsworthiness

Before writing in any format, journalists should be able to discuss what's new in this story, what's the angle for the lead, and why this story is important. They also should be able to check and evaluate the information sources. Some newsrooms have policies about how many sources must be cross-referenced to validate information and if they need two or three to cross-check the other.

Keeping in mind that individual local stations have their own policies, the following sections review some generally accepted checks on information.

Research Check: Is It Accurate?

Whether the news story is true in both concept and detail is the foremost standard of journalism for any medium. Even with the deadline pressure of broadcast and the uncertainty of many untested facts, accuracy should be relentlessly pursued.

Any fact is only as good as its source. Sociologist Gaye Tuchman, in her classic *Making News: A Study in the Construction of Reality* (New York: Free Press, 1978), describes the method journalists use to verify facts as "the web of facticity," meaning that facts are perceived as wholly or partially true because they either come from an authoritative and reliable source or are compared to other "facts" already believed valid. Edward Jay Epstein, in his *Between Fact and Fiction: The Problem of Journalism* (New York: Vintage, 1975), demonstrates how journalists pass along unchecked and wrong information from long-held and traditional sources, based solely on the authority of a single source. Dubious sources are often left unqualified as such in the story.

A troublesome problem lies within the portions of recorded interviews, speeches, and news conferences that are chosen for use in stories ("actualities" in radio and "soundbites" in TV). Often, the speakers make outrageous claims that are hard or impossible to verify before deadlines. Statements are assumed to be true because the interviewees or speakers claim them to be true. The broadcast journalist should put these claims into some perspective and should not build stories around single nonverifiable charges, even if made by a reliable source at a public news conference.

Television news adds another dimension. Because it is photojournalism, television presents the visual representation of current events by cutting together sequences of videotape into visual summaries. It is easy for visuals focused on one story element or location to misrepresent other story elements. With every assignment, television journalists should ask themselves: Is the visual summary accurate? For example, do the 20 seconds of video at the protest demonstration constitute a true picture of what went on during the six hours outside a government building?

Research Check: Is It Plausible?

As a journalist, you should have a good idea of the authenticity of the claims made or news presented in the story.

Your story is only as good as your sources. It is always wise to ask: Do I have the strongest sources for this information? Are you using reliable primary sources, qualified experts, actual eyewitnesses? Or are you talking to someone who heard it from someone who heard it from someone?

Research Check: Is It Fair?

Fairness is an attempt to put, with equal passion and competence, all sides of the story before the audience. It is a sincere recognition of the intelligence of your listeners and viewers—letting them decide what's right and what's wrong, what's good and what's bad.

Is this hope naive? Many argue fairness will never happen, and they're partially right. There's an old debate about whether a journalist can really set aside personal values, prejudices, or previous knowledge of persons or events. As with accuracy, fairness in every story is a goal worth pursuing.

Now Add Perspective

A shared objective in both print and broadcast involves the injection of perspective—the overview—into the story. Journalists do this by tying in old stories, historical facts, new angles, sidebars, and their own personal memories of the same story. Relating the newest breaking events to trends is essential to good reporting but must be undertaken with caution. Faulty memories, slipshod filing systems, or untrustworthy Internet information can add unbalanced perspective and can damage the story's credibility.

Sensational Language/Loaded Words

The addition of opinionated adjectives, sensational adverbs, powerful verbs, zany bits of narrative, or the bizarre opinions of secondary sources—all these constitute dangerous ground for the journalist. Quite often the commonly used adjective in front of a firm's name, for example, the "troubled Hillview bank," or even repeated comments by others such as "neighbors said Wilson was strange and often crept through front yards like a burglar," are misrepresentations we wouldn't want used against ourselves.

This problem also shows up in soundbites chosen for the newscast. Colorful language is more of a danger for broadcast journalists who must write in colloquial language, which is not as precise as most printed text.

More Problems

Review this story and copyedit it. Review this copy for accuracy, fairness, plausibility, the scope of the story, number style, and all other considerations raised in this chapter.

DRUG/jnh/1pm

SCIENTISTS AT MONOPOLY LABS IN FRANCE ARE SAYING A NEW ANTI-RASH DRUG IS GIVING EXCITING RESULTS.

SUFFERERS FROM CRIPPLING BOUTS OF POISON OAK AND POISON IVY SHOULD REJOICE. THEIR SUFFERING MAY END SOON.

IN THREE TESTS OVER SIX WEEKS...POISON OAK RASHES ON 4,237 RATS WERE AFFECTED 40% OF THE TIME FOR THE ALPHA TEST SEQUENCE AND 21% OF THE TIME FOR THE BETA TEST SEQUENCE. THIS LED RESEARCHERS TO A 3 OUT OF TEN PROBABILITY THAT THE NEW OINTMENT IS EFFECTIVE...AT LEAST ON RATS.

HUMAN CLINICAL TESTING BEGINS SOON.

LIBEL, SLANDER, AND INVASION OF PRIVACY

Writers, reporters, and copyeditors should be on the lookout for stories that might injure someone with defamatory information. Although news staffers may not know the finer points of the law, it is important to know when to start worrying about a phrase, a sentence, or an entire item. If the story looks questionable, they should consult the news director or a company lawyer.

To begin with, defamation laws are state laws, and differ across the country. (Ideally, the station should provide a summary of local statutes.) Some general concepts, however, apply throughout.

Three concerns in defamation are libel, slander, and invasion of privacy. Libel (and slander in many cases) is false information, broadcast to an audience of more than one, that identifies someone and injures their reputation, relationships, or occupation. Usually, libel is written information; however, many states accept scripted broadcast material, even if it was spoken on the air, as libel. The consequences of libel can be quite severe, and libel judgments against small operations could put a radio or television station out of business.

In some states, slander is basically the same as libel, except that it is spoken. In other states, it is considered to be impromptu speech, and carries lesser weight in court than libel.

Invasion of privacy involves a true story that identifies and harms. It covers the areas of private space intrusion, publication of private matters, putting a person in a false light, and the right to publicity. Generally, the categories concerning newswriters are the publication of private matters, most notably a criminal past, and putting a person in a false light. Federal courts have ruled that anything on the public record, such as arrests and court decisions, even if a number of years old, may be reported. You will run into trouble, however, when your story about someone's past includes material from unofficial sources. To defend against invasion of privacy, reporters have to prove the newsworthiness of the material.

Why Study Libel at All?

Two good sets of reasons stand out. First, consider the defensive ones. You could save someone's reputation by heading off a flawed and poorly researched story. This is worth the effort because reputations—even those of people not immediately likeable—are hard to repair after they have been publicly trashed.

Second, and still a bit on the defensive side, you can stay out of court and avoid litigation. This saves you time (going to court is tedious and may take months) and in the end, you also can save your job and even your station.

Last, keep in mind the aggressive reason. Know the libel laws and you'll know when you are in the right and can push a story or an investigation. Threats of libel suits may send you to the lawyers, but they won't automatically stifle the controversial stories.

When Does Libel Exist?

Certain general conditions have to exist for libel to occur in most cases.

Identification. Even if accidental, a verbal or visual identification of a person to the satisfaction of the listeners or viewers is sufficient for the courts. This can also happen if you identify a person as a member of a small, exclusive group; however, in that case, the others in that group may sue too.

Be cautious when working with visuals. A closeup of someone's face on the air while your copy talks about drugs, offensive illnesses, and the like is enough to set off a libel suit—as long as the identification is solid.

Broadcast or publication. All you have to do is broadcast the libelous material to at least one person.

Injury or harm. This is what it's all about. If your story could injure a person's reputation or his or her ability to have friends or pursue a profession, it could be libelous. In the same fashion, you can libel a corporation and injure its ability to do business.

Negligence or malice. This is one of those odd twists. Quite likely, if the mistake gets on the air, you will already have been negligent. Negligence, however, is different from malice. If you are simply negligent, it's quite unlikely there will be a large-sized damage award. But if the plaintiff proves malice, a lot of money could change hands.

In a sense, malice is serious negligence. It involves two situations. The first, called intent, means the reporter planned to harm the individual in the story, no matter what the truth. It brings up the old sarcastic news adage "Don't let the facts get in the way of a good story."

It is more likely that a second definition of malice will be involved—that you did not apply normal news-gathering practices to this story. This could mean failing to consult multiple sources, for example, or ignoring research. This type of malice is generally proven by testimony that you just didn't bother to try hard enough to find out whether your information was true or not.

If malice is proven, private persons who have already proven libel can ask for additional multimillion-dollar punitive damages. Even more in damages can be at stake if public persons can sue you for libel about stories involving their public duties.

How Do you Tell a Private Person From a Public Person?

Courts have decided there are two general classes of people who may sue for libel. There are those who have remained out of the public eye, carrying on their lives without seeking public office or publicity. These are private people. The majority of the people you interact with when gathering news are private citizens. When false and damaging information is broadcast about private persons, they are likely to collect damages.

But so-called public persons are viewed with a different standard. The courts have ruled there must be some leeway for news reporters who constantly work with information about persons who voluntarily or involuntarily ended up in the public eye. Sometimes stories, although based upon proven sources, will be wrong. Therefore, less stringent standards are applied when public persons sue for libel. Even if the story is not true, public persons must prove malice was involved.

The line separating a public and private person is ill-defined. The courts have gone back and forth over the years, and there is no set legal definition. Usually, if a person voluntarily inserts himself or herself into the public eye (for example, if a candidate runs for office or a massive amount of publicity is put out about some entertainment star), that person can be considered a public person.

Someone can also involuntarily move into the public arena by becoming involved in an unexpected but highly public event. The court ruled that the man who slapped the gun hand of a suspect shooting at then President Gerald Ford had become a public person for a short time, and that the normal investigation into elements of his private life were acceptable pursuits of journalism. An invasion of privacy suit by the man was thrown out for that reason. On the other hand, just because someone is related to a public official doesn't make him or her a public person.

How About Consent?

What if a person agreed to an interview, then libeled 15 individuals in the answers to your questions. If the interview is cut into a story and goes out on the newscast, who is the responsible party? Who is going to get sued?

Anything you broadcast is your responsibility. If you broadcast a libelous statement, and leave it as the sole reference, without any other sources or perspective, then you and your station might be heading to court. Because someone says something in an interview doesn't mean that it is legal or truthful. You have the right to use that quote, but also the responsibility to report on its accuracy.

Privileged Situations

Privilege here refers to giving fair and accurate accounts of the community's official business. If you are reporting the actions in a privileged situation (for example, any official court proceeding or publicly assembled federal, state, or municipal government body), you are a surrogate for the public and may report what went on, even if what happened was libelous. Therefore if one lawmaker referred to another in a false and damaging way, you may report it, as long as it is an accurate account.

Keep in mind one caution, though. This "privilege" does not apply to statements outside the courtroom or outside the legislative chambers or the city council meeting room. Even if you give a fair and accurate account of a news conference in the hallway after the event, the shield of privilege is gone.

Statute of Limitations

Many states have a set time in which the libel or slander must be contested. In California, it is a year from the date of the libel.

Still Worried?

It is often impossible for reporters, untrained in the law, to be up-to-date on all defamation laws. When a question arises, check with the executive producer, the news director, or the station attorneys. Be prepared to back up your angle with facts, multisource research, and a knowledge of the law. Otherwise you may get an overcautious decision from these people, who know all too well what a libel suit can do to the station.

(((**EXERCISE 2-D**)))

Libel #1

Examine this story for libel. Circle any possible problems.

——— O/C   THE BLUE BEACH BOARD OF EDUCATION TODAY REMOVED AN ELEMENTARY SCHOOL PRINCIPAL FOR CHARGES OF CHILD ABUSE.

BOARD OFFICIALS WOULDN'T REVEAL THE NAME OF THE PRINCIPAL...SAYING ONLY THAT SHE WORKED IN ONE OF FOUR PINE DISTRICT SCHOOLS.

THE BOARD STATEMENT SAYS PARENTS HAD CHARGED THE PRINCIPAL WITH ABUSING CHILDREN AFTER SCHOOL HOURS IN HER OFFICE.

TWO WEEKS AGO...IRATE PARENTS AT MILLDOWN SCHOOL INTERRUPTED A BOARD MEETING TO COMPLAIN ABOUT PRINCIPAL LOUISE GITTLER.

THE DISTRICT ATTORNEY'S OFFICE HAS NOT FILED CHARGES.

(# # #)

Libel #2

Examine this story for libel. Circle any possible problems.

——— O/C   THE LEAD SINGER OF THE MUSIC GROUP
THE WANTON TWITS IS SAYING THE BAND
WON'T APPEAR IN THE MARCH THIRD BIG
STEEL CONCERT.

LEICESTER AREA FANS HAVE ALREADY
BOUGHT NINE-THOUSAND TICKETS TO THE
TWITS CONCERT...SOMETIMES PAYING AS
MUCH AS 35-DOLLARS PER TICKET.

TWITS MANAGER AND SINGER AAZY PERCH
SAYS PROMOTER LYLE LEFEVER STOLE MONEY
FROM THEM...ROUGHED THEM UP...AND GAVE
THEM DRUGS DURING CONTRACT TALKS.

LEFEVER WAS NOT AVAILABLE FOR
COMMENT.

(# # #)

Invasion of Privacy

Examine this story for invasion of privacy. Discuss in class what you think are areas of concern.

——— O/C   A MAN WHO WANTS TO BE THE NEW DAYCARE COORDINATOR OF ROWART COUNTY HAS A LONG CRIMINAL RECORD.

RICHARD SEWELL ADMITTED THE CHARGES THIS AFTERNOON.

OLD NEWSPAPER ACCOUNTS SAY THE ARRESTS ALL HAPPENED MORE THAN 10-YEARS AGO AND INVOLVED BAD CHECKS AND CREDIT CARDS.

SEWELL SAYS NONE OF THE ARRESTS HAD GONE TO COURT AND SOLUTIONS HAD BEEN WORKED OUT WITH THE BANKS.

ANOTHER CANDIDATE FOR THE JOB MADE THE CHARGES PUBLIC.

READ IT ALOUD!

Although broadcast newsrooms often look like any other office area, there is a subtle difference. Most reporters and writers typing at keyboards appear to be talking to themselves. In most cases, they are finishing the most important step in broadcast writing—reading the final version aloud. That's one way to tell what's awkward and what's not. Read every story aloud.

Computer systems have special function keys to highlight words, but many newscasters still add marks to the paper copy. They use individual marks, underlining, and slashes to add emphasis, or short arrows to indicate a change in voice pitch. All this, however, must be reflected in changes to the prompter copy too. Each prompter system has a method to highlight and insert these marks.

Here's an example of marked copy:

SURVEY/jnh/3:30pm

A NEW <u>SURVEY</u> IS REPORTING HIGH SCHOOL STUDENTS WILL HAVE SEEN AT LEAST <u>20-THOU-SAND MURDERS</u> // IN THE MOVIES AND ON TV // BY THE TIME THEY ENTER COLLEGE.

THE REPORT FROM THE ANNENBERG SCHOOL OF COMMUNICATIONS AT PENN STATE SAYS THE <u>EXPOSURE</u> TO MANY VIOLENT ACTS COULD <u>DAMAGE THEIR PERSONALITIES</u>...AND <u>DESENSITIZE THEM</u> TO COMMON KINDNESS.

(# # #)

Punctuation and Rehearsal Marks

Review this story for correct punctuation and put in rehearsal marks for reading.

RECORD/jnh/6pm

AN OREGON MAN IN A 45-FOOT SAILBOAT REACHED BOSTON HARBOR ON WEDNESDAY...BREAKING A 140-YEAR-OLD RECORD FOR THE TRIP FROM SAN FRANCISCO.

THE LONE SAILOR...DALE CREST...ENDURED STORMY SEAS AND GALE FORCE WINDS ON THE EAST COAST BUT STILL FINISHED IN 69 DAYS...MORE THAN SEVEN DAYS FASTER THAN THE PREVIOUS RECORD.

CREST SAID HIS TRIP WAS EXHAUSTING AND DANGEROUS AND HE WASN'T GOING TO TRY—QUOTE—TO DO SOMETHING THAT STUPID AGAIN.

THE THREE-MASTED CLIPPER SHIP NORTHERN LIGHT HELD THE PREVIOUS RECORD. THAT SHIP MADE THE TRIP IN 76 DAYS...OVER ONE HUNDRED YEARS AGO.

(# # #)

CHAPTER SUMMARY

Broadcast scripts require attention to standards and style. The copy must be accurate, fair, and comprehensive. Writers must also include technical details for smooth studio production. Writers must also watch sentence length, details, and number form to keep the copy readable. They must be knowledgeable about libel, slander, and invasion of privacy laws and avoid those faults—while continuing to press stories that need to be told. A final check of good writing is to read the story aloud.

3

The Shift From Print to Effective Broadcast Copy

CHAPTER PREVIEW

This chapter covers many of the structural changes necessary to convert prose to broadcast writing, including the use of the active voice; concise verbs, adjectives, and phrases; attribution; and multiple tenses. The problems of misused phrases, double-referenced pronouns, awkwardly long introductory phrases, and midsentence nested phrases are also explored.

Repetition, which is to be avoided in many situations, can be a valuable tool, as are elliptical or half-completed sentences. Exercises provide a test for skills in this chapter.

GLOSSARY

ACTIVE VOICE Verb form in which the thing of person responsible for the action precedes the verb.

ATTRIBUTION A phrase or sentence that reveals the source of your information for a news story. Attribution helps establish credibility.

ELLIPTICAL SENTENCES A sentence fragment that is designed to mimic speech patterns and that usually is missing either the subject or verb. Elliptical sentences are sometimes used in broadcast news scripts.

NESTED PHRASES Midsentence phrases that break up the continuity of the sentence elements, usually the subject and verb.

PASSIVE VOICE Verb form in which the thing or person responsible for the action follows the verb.

READER The most frequently used broadcast format, it is a story—usually short and under 40 seconds—read by the newscaster without accompanying sound, actualities, or videotape. Also called a *read*, a *live*, a *live-er*, or a *copy story.*

USE STRONG, CONCISE WORDS AND PHRASES

Broadcast writers must make an effort to use short, simple words. Literary writing allows the use of longer, often obscure verbs and adjectives, but conversational writing has other needs. Verbs should be positive and in the most direct form; adjectives should be short and clear; and writers should pare phrases down to the essentials.

Wordy Verb Forms

Look for ways to express action clearly and simply. Review the verb and infinitive forms to see whether there is a more simple verb or infinitive to convey the same idea and make the sentence easier to understand.

> COMPLEX: THEY VOTED <u>TO TERMINATE THE CONSTRUCTION</u> OF THE BRIDGE.

Instead, you could have written:

> SIMPLE: THEY VOTED <u>TO STOP BUILDING</u> THE BRIDGE.

Negative Verbs

Quite often, long negative verbs provide a similar opportunity. Look for positive replacements for negative verb forms. Here's an example:

> NEGATIVE: THREE OTHER CONVICTS <u>DECIDED NOT TO ESCAPE</u> ALONG WITH THE FIRST GROUP

A more direct verb construction would be:

> POSITIVE: THREE OTHER CONVICTS DECIDED <u>TO STAY PUT</u>.

As you can see, the sentence is stronger and more direct with the positive verb form. Here's an exercise to change some lengthy verbs and simplify them. Try the examples.

Revising Long or Negative Verbs or Infinitives

Review these examples. Shorten and simplify the verbs or infinitive forms and change negative ones to positive.

Sample:

OVER 200 DINERS BECAME ILL AFTER <u>INGESTING</u> THE SPOILED FOOD.

That can be changed to:
OVER 200 DINERS BECAME ILL AFTER <u>EATING</u> THE SPOILED FOOD.

1. ENGINEERS PLAN TO <u>OPERATIONALIZE</u> THE PLANT THIS WEEK.

2. THE COUNTY WILL <u>NOT PROHIBIT</u> BUILDING PERMITS.

3. THE HEALTH DEPARTMENT IS PROPOSING <u>TO IMPART</u> THE FLU SHOTS TUESDAY.

4. THE STORM <u>INUNDATED</u> THE STREETS OF STEELTOWN.

5. THE TOWN COUNCIL ADVISED MERCHANTS TO NOT PAY ATTENTION TO THE CONTROVERSY.

6. NEW STATE LAWS PROSCRIBE OVERNIGHT CAMPING IN THE PARKS.

7. THE JURY CONVICTED THE DEFENDANT OF EAVESDROPPING ON HIS COWORKERS.

8. AIR TRAVELERS WILL CONFRONT LONG DELAYS THIS WEEKEND.

9. THE PERPETRATOR DEPARTED THE BUILDING THROUGH THE BACK DOOR.

10. SPRING IS HERE...AND IT IS A TIME TO METAMORPHOSE ONE'S ATTENTION TO GOOD WEATHER.

11. THE PILOTS' UNION EMBRACED THE NEW CONTRACT PROPOSAL.

Adjectives

For adjectives, the advice is much the same as for verbs: Keep it simple. Use direct, strong words and rework hyphenated adjectives. For instance, change *poverty-stricken* to poor and change *collective* effort to joint effort.

Find shorter, more powerful adjectives in the following exercise.

(((**EXERCISE 3-A2**)))

Replacing Overwrought Adjectives

Review these examples. Replace adjectives which are unnecessarily long.

Sample:

THE COURT RULED HOUSING CONDITIONS WERE <u>JERRY-BUILT</u>.

Reworked, it might say:

THE COURT RULED HOUSING CONDITIONS WERE <u>SHODDY</u>.

1. THE DEFENDANT ADMITTED HE WAS <u>REMORSEFUL</u>.

2. THE NEWLY MODIFIED HOME APPEARED <u>GARGANTUAN</u>.

3. THE LANDLORD WAS PROSPEROUS.

4. AN IMPRACTICABLE JOURNEY WAS STILL AHEAD.

5. THE COAST GUARD SAID THE TANKER HAD AN ILLEGITIMATE CARGO.

6. DEBATE JUDGES CHOSE THE SUPERLATIVE PUBLIC SPEAKER.

Phrases

Phrases are often unneeded and can be removed without changing the clarity or meaning of the sentence. In many cases, the writer might be using six words where one might do. Here's an example:

THE COUNCIL VOTED TO PROCEED WITH RECONSTRUCTION OF THE STREETS...

Change that to

THE COUNCIL VOTED TO FIX THE STREETS...

Now try to rewrite this next story, taking out unnecessary phrases.

((• EXERCISE 3-B •))

Rewriting for Phrases

THE TOWN COUNCIL MEMBERS HAD TO STAY FOR THE LATE-NIGHT SESSION OF THE COUNCIL THAT RAN INTO THE WEE HOURS OF THE MORNING.

FINALLY...THEY VOTED AS A GROUP TO MODIFY THE TAX STRUCTURE IN DOWNY FALLS AND ALLOW SOME OF THE MONEY FROM TAXES TO GO INTO A CITY FUND TO REPAIR THE STREETS OF THE CITY.

Word Variety

It goes without saying that, if possible, a good writer avoids repeating the same words in a sentence or continuous sentences. Good newswriters should always be on the lookout for this type of structure and ways to avoid it.

Example:

THE FIRE TRUCKS ARRIVED ON ELM STREET AS THE FIRE LEAPED OUT THE FIRST FLOOR WINDOWS OF THE RESIDENCE HOTEL.
FIREFIGHTERS QUICKLY PULLED RESIDENTS FROM THE FIRE'S PATH AND THEN BATTLED THE FIRE FOR THE NEXT HOUR.
THE FIRE WAS OUT AT SIX P-M.

Special Case of the Verb To Say.   Although students are urged to find synonyms for words to add variety, the verb *say* or *said* is one word for which you usually don't need a synonym. Alternatives such as *assert, declare, state, pronounce, vocalize, exclaim,* or *voice* are stodgy, awkward and often color the delivery of the sentence. Repeat the verb *say* as often as you like. Here are two paragraphs: The first uses various synonyms. The second uses repetition of the verb *to say.*

MARKER/Jnh/6pm

POLICE SAY THE SUSPECT TURNED

AROUND...REACHED FOR THE FELT-TIPPED

PEN...AND MARKED THE WALLS.

OFFICIALS STATED HE KNEW EXACTLY WHAT

HE WAS DOING.

THE PROSECUTOR DECLARED SHE'LL ASK FOR

A TRIAL.

Instead, you can change that to the following:

MARKER/jnh/6pm

POLICE SAY THE SUSPECT TURNED AROUND...

REACHED FOR THE FELT-TIPPED PEN...AND

MARKED THE WALLS.

OFFICIALS SAID HE KNEW EXACTLY WHAT HE

WAS DOING. THE PROSECUTOR SAID SHE'LL ASK

FOR A TRIAL.

Simplify the Story

Examine these stories for complex words, negative verbs, and unneeded phrases. Rewrite if needed.

TWELVE MEMBERS OF THE SHERIFF'S SWAT TEAM PROVIDED HELPFUL ASSISTANCE DURING THE DANGEROUS APPREHENSION OF THE BELLIGERENT SUSPECT...ONE JOHN E. JUDD...29...OF BELLEVILLE.

———

THE VIOLENT STANDOFF TRANSFORMED A NORMALLY TRANQUIL AND PICTURESQUE AGRICULTURAL TOWN INTO A SUSPICIOUS COMMUNITY OF FEAR.

———

THE EXHILARATED SCIENTISTS WERE EXCITED BUT CAUTIOUS AT THE SAME MOMENT...EXPLAINING THAT THE INNOVATIVE AND TRAILBLAZING DISCOVERY WAS UNTESTED.

THEY SAID THAT WHILE THEY DIDN'T WANT TO NOT NOTIFY THE PUBLIC OF THE NEWS...THEY WERE WORRIED THEY MIGHT UNDULY SCARE THEM.

Better Choices

Try your hand at seeing how few words you can use to relate the same idea. Clarify the stories below by deleting unnecessary words and replacing complex words with simpler ones.

TWO AS YET UNIDENTIFIED MEN AT THE STARLIGHT MOTEL SUFFERED SERIOUS AND NEAR FATAL INJURIES IN SPECTACULAR FALLS FROM SECOND FLOOR BALCONIES TO THE GROUND FLOOR BELOW.

TREASURE HUNTERS WORKING THE PLACID BLUE WATERS OF THE CARIBBEAN SEA ARE DECLARING THAT THEY HAVE CERTAINLY FOUND THE REMAINS OF A SUNKEN 16TH CENTURY SPANISH FLEET GALLEON CALLED...LA GORDITA DE ORO.

JUDGE JOSHUA DUGAN'S EXCEEDINGLY COMPLEX AND INVOLVED DECISION CAME JUST THREE WEEKS AFTER THE LAWYERS FILED THE FIRST MOTION.

THE STATE OF DELAWARE WAS THE ONLY STATE TO REFUSE TO PARTICIPATE IN THE FEDERAL GOVERNMENT'S NATIONAL POLICE PROTECTION ACT GRANT PROGRAM.

Comprehensive

Examine this story for verb and adjective complexity and unneeded phrases. Copyedit.

TEST SCORES FOR THE STATE'S KIDS OF SCHOOL AGE ARE ELEVATED UP IN MANY DIFFERENT AREAS IN THE LATEST STATEWIDE ACHIEVEMENT EVALUATION TEST EXAMS.

STATE SUPERINTENDENT OF SCHOOLS ROGER B. CARNS SAID INNOVATIVE AND NOVEL TITLE FOUR FUNDED PROGRAMS THAT RETURNED TO FUNDAMENTAL BASIC CONCEPTS OF EDUCATION COULD BE CITED AS RESPONSIBLE FOR THE GAIN.

LOCAL SCHOOL OFFICIALS ONCE AGAIN REITERATED THAT ASSESSMENT DECLARING THE NEW PROGRAM IS WORKING...

OFFICIALS ALSO STATED THEY WOULD PURSUE OTHER REFORMS...INCLUDING SHRINKING CLASS SIZE AND ADDING THOSE ENRICHMENT CLASSES LIKE ART AND MUSIC.

ELLIPTICAL SENTENCES

Because broadcast writers aim to mimic speech patterns, news copy may have elliptical sentences—sentence fragments with implied but unspoken words or phrases. Elliptical sentences help to keep the word count down and to reinforce conversational patterns. Here's an example:

> IT'S THAT TIME OF YEAR AGAIN...TIME FOR PICNICS...FRIVOLITY...
> TRIPS TO THE BEACH.
> IT'S SUMMER. THAT MEANS RELAXATION. HERE'S A REPORT.

In the previous example, many connective words and even nouns are left out, but the intent is still understood.

The speech pattern and delivery of a legendary radio news reporter is the classic example. One of his stories might go something like this.

> IN NEW JERSEY. A TRAGEDY. BUT ONE UNLIKE OTHERS. A MAN...
> DESPONDENT...HE TRIED TO COMMIT SUICIDE. BOUGHT A GUN. PUT
> THE BARREL TO HIS HEAD. PULLED THE TRIGGER.
> DIDN'T WORK. HE MISSED. THE BULLET HIT THE WATER HEATER. IT
> BLEW UP AND BURNED THE MAN'S HOUSE DOWN.

Modern sportscasters also get in on the fun.

> BASEBALL. HITS. HOMERUNS. OUTS. LOSERS. LET'S SEE THE VIDEOTAPE.

That's how elliptical it can get. New writers should avoid overusing this style, but it doesn't hurt to fashion the occasional elliptical sentence to give a conversational feeling to the writing. Here's another example:

> ICY NIGHTS ALL THIS WEEK.
> THE FIRST ONES THIS YEAR.
> MAYBE AN EARLY WINTER.
> ALL OF IT AN EMBARRASSING SURPRISE FOR DOWNY FALLS OFFI-
> CIALS WHO HAVEN'T OPENED UP THE SHELTERS YET.
> HOMELESS ACTIVISTS WANT IMMEDIATE ACTION.
> BUT CITY WORKERS SAY THEY NEED TWO MORE WEEKS UNTIL THE
> SHELTERS ARE READY.

Eliminating Words and Phrases

Examine this story for elliptical possibilities. Revise it by removing phrases or rewriting.

ELECTION/jnh/6pm

CITIZENS IN BALLARD COUNTY MADE SURE IN THE ELECTION LAST NIGHT THAT THE REFORM FORCES IN THE COUNTY WOULD BE TAKING OVER THE REINS OF GOVERNMENT.

VOTERS SENT 12-INCUMBENTS PACKING...A SURE SIGN THEY WERE UPSET WITH THE STATUS QUO AT THIS TIME.

THE MOST PROMINENT OFFICE HOLDER TO LOSE HIS SEAT IN THE COUNTY IN THIS ELECTION WAS SHERIFF BRIAN CANDALARIO. COUNTY MANAGER CARLTON FRANKLIN SQUEAKED BY WITH A NARROW WIN BY A VERY SMALL MARGIN.

ATTRIBUTION

Attribution is the inclusion of source identification to establish credibility or doubt in your story. Attribution poses two questions for broadcast writers: Where should it be placed and when should it be used? The first answer is easy—attribution should, and usually does, go first. But the second question involves many individual judgments.

When to Use Attribution

Below are suggestions to help you determine when attribution is appropriate.

Use It for Credibility.   By naming your sources of information, you enable your viewers or listeners to judge the value of your facts. The audience knows a foreign policy statement that originates at the White House has more credibility than a foreign policy statement from the manager of the local supermarket. In stories with contested facts, attributions let the audience decide about credibility.

Use It to Show Doubt.   Similarly, if you have doubts about the quality of the information, it is traditional journalistic practice to alert the audience to this fact. Anonymous telephone information inserted in a story should be identified as such. Exclusive stories from other media should credit those organizations, unless you can cross-check the information. Also, the source for any information from a suspect organization, one with a big name but only four members, must be identified.

Use it to Support Opinion.   Attribution is clearly needed if what you are reporting is opinion or speculation.

Shorten Attribution or Discard It to Save Space.   Use of attribution in broadcast is not the same as in print. Because story space is severely limited in newscasts, it is often necessary to condense the source of information or to eliminate it altogether. In broadcast, long government titles are often shortened to "officials" or "authorities," especially when that information is of routine value.

Often, a writer might exclude the reference altogether, as in the case of routine sources that mean little to the outcome of the story. If the Consumer Price Index goes up or down, there is little question where the information comes from, so why bother with the attribution?

When to Always Use Attribution.   Always use attribution in crime stories. Make a point of using attribution to demonstrate that you are relying on authoritative sources. When describing a crime to which a person's name may be linked, it is irresponsible not to use attribution.

Where to Put Attribution

Although newspaper and wire service copy traditionally puts the attribution at the end of a sentence, broadcast puts it first. Here's an example of print placement.

THE UNITED STATES AND FRANCE WILL SOON MEET IN NEW NEGO-TIATIONS OVER THE GATT TRADE AGREEMENTS, ACCORDING TO A HIGHLY PLACED STATE DEPARTMENT SOURCE.

In broadcast, the attribution always, always goes first.

A STATE DEPARTMENT OFFICIAL IS SAYING THE U-S AND FRANCE WILL MEET TO DISCUSS TRADE AGREEMENTS.

Placing the attribution first allows the audience a chance to judge source credibility as the facts are heard, rather than waiting for a delayed attribution.

Spotting Trouble

Examine these stories for attribution problems. Be prepared to discuss if you would use the attribution and how it might be written.

A NATIONAL UNION OFFICIAL IS SAYING THAT ALL GROCERY CLERKS SHOULD GET AT LEAST SIX WEEKS VACATION.

———

ALL STATE TROOPERS WILL RECEIVE ETHICS COUNSELING IN THE WAKE OF THE SEX SCANDALS...ACCORDING TO STATE POLICE CHIEF RAUL RAMIREZ.

———

AN EARTHQUAKE SHOOK THE TRI-CITY AREA THIS MORN-ING...REGISTERING THREE-POINT-FOUR ON THE RICHTER SCALE...ACCORDING TO THE GEOLOGICAL SERVICE.

———

THE SHORELINE REFINERY HAS BEEN RELEASING UNTREATED CHEMICALS DIRECTLY INTO THE MARSHY WET-LANDS...ACCORDING TO THE SAVE THE MARSH COMMITTEE.

———

BUGS BUNNY WILL BE 50-YEARS-OLD TOMORROW...A CARTOON OFFICIAL SAID.

More Attribution Exercises

Examine these stories for attribution problems. Eliminate the attribution or restructure the sentences for broadcast style.

THE HIGHWAY DEATH TOLL SOARED TO 500 OVER THE LABOR DAY WEEKEND...ACCORDING TO A HIGHWAY SAFETY OFFICIAL.

———

THE SUSPECT IS BYRON WALCOTT...ACCORDING TO POLICE.

———

THE GIANT TANKER SPLIT IN TWO OFF CLAMSHELL COVE DURING THE STORM....ACCORDING TO A SPOKESWOMAN FOR THE COAST GUARD.

———

THE NEW PROGRAM SHOULD HELP THE MAYOR'S CAMPAIGN NEXT YEAR...THINK MOST POLITICAL OBSERVERS.

———

THE SINGER WILL APPEAR IN FOUR CONCERTS NEXT AUGUST...ACCORDING TO HER MANAGER.

Comprehensive Review

Examine these sentences for word complexity, wordy verbs, unneeded phrases, and attribution problems. If necessary, restructure the sentences to put them into an effective broadcast style.

THE SAN CRISTOBAL MAYOR ACCEPTED AN ILLEGAL BRIBE DURING NEW CONVENTION CENTER WORK...THE HERALD IS REPORTING TODAY.

———

A TEAM OF DOCTORS AT THE BENTON CAMPUS STATE UNIVERSITY MEDICAL CENTER WILL ATTEMPT A CROSS SPECIES NERVE TRANSPLANT...HOSPITAL OFFICIALS ARE SAYING.

———

RACE OFFICIALS SAY THE STREETS AND AVENUES WILL BE CROWDED AND JAMMED WITH UPWARDS OF 40-THOUSAND RUNNERS IN TOMORROW'S MUSCULAR DYSTROPHY MARATHON.

———

THOUSANDS OF SQUARE DANCING FANATICS WILL SOON FILL THE BALLROOMS OF KANSAS CITY'S BIG HOTELS AT THE ANNUAL NATIONAL DANCE COMPETITION.

ACTIVE AND PASSIVE VERBS

The passive voice, in which the thing or person responsible for the action appears after the verb, is the most common roadblock for beginning broadcast writers. Using passive voice is a leftover from schoolwork that trained us to place the most important word or event at the beginning of the sentence. Following this rule, in writing a story about a bank robbery in which *bank* is the most important word, we naturally insert the word *bank* somewhere in the first three words of the sentence "The bank was robbed by the lone gunman." Here the verb is in the passive voice, because the action was done to the bank not by the bank.

In broadcast, however, it is important to construct a smooth sentence flow. Start the sentence with the persons or objects that did the action, even if a word such as *bank* is still the most important item. By turning the sentence around, you get "The lone gunman robbed the bank." It is shorter and more direct, and it is in the active voice. Broadcast writers make every attempt to keep all the verbs in active rather than passive voice.

Be careful not to confuse voice with tense. Voice has nothing to do with when the action happened, only with the placement of who or what is responsible for the action in relation to the verb.

Changing the Voice

There are cues to alert you to passive voice. In the sentence "The mail carrier was bitten by the dog," the dog is obviously responsible for the action but the word *dog* comes after the verb. The *was* and *by* are clues that passive voice was used.

Turning a sentence around is easy. Here are some passive voice constructions and the same sentences after the active voice has been used.

Passive: The toxic spill was spotted by the rangers.

Active: The rangers spotted the toxic spill.

Passive: The family was forced to flee by the flood.

Active: The flood forced the family to flee.

In each case, the cues are obvious—*was* and *by*. Notice also that the sentence that is in active voice is shorter and the action flows more smoothly. You are saving words and time.

Replacing Passive Voice

Change any passive voice verbs to active.

MILLIONS OF DOLLARS WORTH OF ARMS HAVE BEEN SHIPPED TO THE TERRORISTS BY THE NEW GOVERNMENT OF ARGENTINA.

———————

THREE HOMES AND A SCHOOL ARE BEING THREATENED BY GRASS FIRES OUTSIDE OF TUCSON.

———————

OVER 100 WORKERS AT THE XERXES METALS PLANT WILL BE LAID OFF BY THE COMPANY BEGINNING NEXT WEDNESDAY.

———————

THE FAMOUS JET CAR USED IN THE BATMAN SERIES WAS AMONG 50 AUCTIONED OFF IN CHICAGO BY A COLLECTOR.

———————

THE FOUR SURFERS WERE ATTACKED BY A GREAT WHITE SHARK OFF THE SANTA CRUZ COAST.

———————

THE RECORD WAS BROKEN BY AMTRAK'S NEW HIGH-SPEED TRAIN.

Rewrite to Active Voice

Circle examples of passive voice in the story below. On a separate page, using correct format, rewrite this story.

ABANDON/jnh/11pm

    THE SUNDAY NEWS HAS LEARNED A MOVE IS BEING MADE BY CLAY COUNTY OFFICIALS TO PREVENT CONSTRUCTION OF THE NEW MAIN SEWER PROJECT.

    THE CONTRACTORS WILL BE ASKED TO STOP THE PRELIMINARY WORK.

    SO FAR...ONLY SURVEYS HAVE BEEN DONE.

    SOURCES SAY THE FEDERAL GOVERNMENT HAS CUT BACK THE GRANTS...AND NOW BILLS FOR THIS PROJECT CAN NO LONGER BE PAID BY THE COUNTY.

    AND IN AN ODD TWIST...COUNTY OFFICIALS SAY THAT IF THE PROJECT IS STOPPED...TOXIC CLEANUP GRANTS TO CLAY COUNTY FOR OTHER PROJECTS WILL BE STOPPED BY THE FEDERAL GOVERNMENT.

MORE EFFECTIVE VERB FORMS

Verbs that often are correct might sometimes need some stronger phrasing. For instance, instead of using the simple present tense, use the participial form with an "ing" ending. Here's an example:

BANKS CHARGE 12-PERCENT INTEREST FOR THREE MONTHS ON THE CONTROVERSIAL LOANS.

To strengthen the verb, write

BANKS ARE CHARGING 12-PERCENT INTEREST FOR THREE MONTHS ON THE CONTROVERSIAL LOANS.

In the same way, the present perfect verb form often makes a more dynamic verb than the simple past. You do this by adding auxiliary verbs to the form. Here's an example:

RESCUERS PULLED THE DAMAGED TRACTOR UP THE LEVEE WALL.

To add emphasis, say

RESCUERS HAVE PULLED THE DAMAGED TRACTOR UP THE LEVEE WALL.

Is This Action an On-going Policy?

Because broadcast provides the latest material, it is always necessary to look for the update. In many cases, especially in the areas of policies and programs, you'll be describing a continuing action, not one that is completed. For all practical purposes, the best verb form for this one is the present participle, which uses the "ing" ending. Here are a few examples:

WORKERS <u>ARE SEARCHING</u> THE WRECKAGE OF THE AIRLINER TONIGHT, LOOKING FOR...

THE CITY COUNCIL <u>IS BETTING</u> THAT THE NORTH STATE UTILITY GROUP WON'T RAISE THE RATES...

Is This an Action Scheduled for the Future?

In broadcast, the future tense is used often to add perspective to the lead about a future course of action. It is also used at the end of a story to suggest what is expected next in a chronological sequence. In both cases, use the participial "ing" form to add conversational tone to your writing.

In the lead:

THE CITY ATTORNEY WILL BE TAKING THE STATE TO COURT OVER
THE LATEST LAW ON RENT CONTROLS.

At the end of the story:

THE CITY ATTORNEY WILL BE FILING THAT LAWSUIT NEXT WEEK
WHEN THE COURTS REOPEN.

(((**EXERCISE 3-L**)))

Effective Verb Forms

Examine these sentences with an eye to making your verbs more effective. Discuss
if you might rewrite any of the verbs.

FORMS/jnh/6pm

RICHMOND CLOSED ITS PORT AFTER YESTERDAY'S FERRY-
BOAT ACCIDENT.

_____

THE FLOODS THAT SWEPT THROUGH BIRNEY FALLS
YESTERDAY CAUSE PROBLEMS TODAY.

_____

POLITICAL CRITICS SUGGESTED THE SENATOR SHOULD
LAY LOW FOR A WHILE UNTIL THE TAXPAYERS BACKLASH
SUBSIDES.

_____

THE POLICE OFFICER RADIOED FOR BACKUP AFTER SHE
PULLED THE FAMILY FROM THE WRECKED CAR.

_____

PILOTS FROM THE AIR RESCUE SQUADRON HOPE THE
STATE WILL INCREASE THEIR COMPENSATION FOR THE
AVIATION FUEL.

Immediacy Needs

In each case, rewrite the verbs to indicate there is a continuing action or policy. Should you be using the "ing" participial form?

THE ZOO BOARD DECIDED TO GIVE A THREE-MONTH PASS TO EVERYONE WHO ATTENDS TODAY'S EXHIBITION.

———

DOCTORS HOPED THE INJECTIONS LAST NIGHT WILL SAVE THE ELDERLY MAN FROM INFECTION.

———

THE WANDERING WHALE ENTERED THE EAST RIVER ON THURSDAY. MARINE MAMMAL EXPERTS CONTINUED TO WATCH ITS PROGRESS.

———

THE GOVERNMENT DEMANDED THE RECALL AFTER TESTS PROVED THE DOOR LOCKS FAILED IN SEVERAL CRASHES.

———

CRITICS WARNED THE CITY WILL STRUGGLE WITH THE HOMELESS ISSUE FOR THE NEXT FIFTY YEARS.

———

UNIVERSITY OFFICIALS TAKE A WAIT-AND-SEE ATTITUDE AFTER THE COACH'S LATEST OUTBURST.

Comprehensive

Examine these sentences for word complexity, active voice, verb form, and attribution. If necessary, rewrite the sentences.

AMERICANS DISAGREED WITH THE POLICIES OF THEIR GOVERNMENT IN THE SAVINGS AND LOAN SCANDAL... ACCORDING TO A NEW POLL.

—————

IT WAS REPORTED BY THE COUNTY NEWS SERVICE THAT THE ROAD TO EAGLES PASS WAS REOPENED YESTERDAY AFTER THE HUGE MASSIVE SNOWSLIDE ON ROUTE 760 WAS CLEANED OFF BY COUNTY ROAD CREWS.

—————

PRISON OFFICIALS INVESTIGATED THE ESCAPE OF THE TWO CONVICTS. THEIR TUNNEL WAS DISCOVERED YESTERDAY AND GUARDS ON DUTY WERE ASKED TO APPEAR TODAY FOR MORE QUESTIONS.

—————

FIVE MORE OF THE BURIAL SITES WERE FOUND. OFFICIALS PLANNED TO EXCAVATE THEM TOMORROW.

—————

THE SNEERING SUSPECT WALKED QUICKLY OUT OF THE COURTROOM AFTER BOOS BROKE OUT.

COMMON REFERENCE PROBLEMS

The need for tightly condensed broadcast copy often results in misplaced modifying phrases and unclear pronoun references. Any modifying phrase or pronoun that is ambiguous must be cleared up, even at the sacrifice of smooth writing.

Pronouns

Broadcast writers often use pronouns with more than one possible antecedent. If there's doubt about whom the pronoun refers to, rewrite the sentence to repeat the proper name and eliminate the pronoun.

Here is an example of an unclear pronoun reference:

THE GOVERNOR AND THE ASSEMBLY SPEAKER DISCUSSED THE SITUATION. THEN <u>HE</u> MADE A MOVE TO CUT THE BUDGET.

In this example, both the governor and the speaker were men. Therefore, it is necessary to identify the antecedent to the pronoun *he* or the sentence is confusing. Here's the rewrite:

THE GOVERNOR AND THE ASSEMBLY SPEAKER DISCUSSED THE SITUATION...THEN THE <u>GOVERNOR</u> MADE A MOVE TO CUT THE BUDGET.

Here's a second example of unclear reference:

POLICE ARRESTED FIVE MEMBERS OF THE PROTEST GROUP AND SAID THEY ARE EXHAUSTED AFTER SPENDING ALL DAY AT THE DEMONSTRATION.

Again, identify the *they*. Here's the rewrite.

POLICE ARRESTED FIVE MEMBERS OF THE PROTEST GROUP AND SAID THE DEMONSTRATORS ARE TIRED AFTER SPENDING ALL DAY AT THE EVENT.

As you can see, these examples of pronoun misuse are easy to correct. But there are other types of pronoun abuse, including the use of *they're* when writers generalize about a community's experiences or feelings. In the lead sentence, a writer might say

THEY'RE WORRIED IN TACOMA TONIGHT...WORRIED ABOUT...

That's a dubious sociological assumption the writer is making up. If you can, avoid the all-inclusive *they're*.

Pronoun Reference

Correct ambiguous pronoun references in these sentences.

THE SUPREME COURT HAS OVERTURNED A LOWER COURT RULING ON THE DEATH PENALTY. THIS IS CONSIDERED A LANDMARK IN CONSTITUTIONAL LAW.

———————

THE DOG SHOW IS TOUGH ON BOTH JUDGES AND CONTESTANTS. THEY HAVE TO SIT QUIETLY FOR HOURS.

———————

RATS MAY HAVE CARRIED THE PLAGUE IN THE MIDDLE AGES...AND NOW EPIDEMIOLOGISTS ARE SAYING THEY ARE RESPONSIBLE FOR THE MYSTERIOUS ILLNESSES IN NEW MEXICO.

———————

THE SHIP'S OWNERS FIRED THE CAPTAIN AS WELL AS THE FIRST MATE. HE HAD BEEN WITH THE COMPANY FOR ALMOST 35-YEARS.

———————

POLICE STATED THE INJURED CHILD HAD WAITED UNTIL HIS MOTHER WASN'T LOOKING...THEN CRAWLED ON HER KNEES TO A NEARBY AND VERY DANGEROUS UNPROTECTED LIGHT SOCKET.

Misplaced Phrases

Phrases can end up in the wrong place when you jam too much information into one sentence. The so-called dangling modifier gets stuck after the wrong word. Here's an example of a misplaced phrase.

> RAP SINGER G-MAN WILL RECEIVE AN AWARD FOR HUMANITARIAN WORK ON THE TONIGHT SHOW.

Now, where was the humanitarian work done? The best solution is to reorganize the sentence. Here it is.

> RAP SINGER G-MAN WILL APPEAR ON THE TONIGHT SHOW TO RECEIVE AN AWARD FOR HUMANITARIAN WORK.

((• **EXERCISE 3-P** •))

Phrases in Motion

Correct the sentences below that have misplaced phrases.

POLICE SAY THE VICTIM IS IN CRITICAL CONDITION AFTER SUFFERING SIX STAB WOUNDS IN HIS KITCHEN.

———

THE PARK AT THE BEACH...WHICH WILL BE AUCTIONED OFF NEXT WEEK...IS THE FOCUS OF THE PROTEST.

———

THERE IS NEW HOPE FOR A CURE FOR HEART DISEASE WHICH IS WHAT MANY RESEARCHERS HAVE WANTED.

———

EVERYONE SAID THE FOOD AT THE COUNTY VOLUNTEERS AWARDS CEREMONY WAS TASTELESS.

———

THE DUCK L'ORANGE WAS ON THE ELABORATE DINNER MENU THAT THE CHEF HAD WORKED ON ALL DAY.

Comprehensive

Correct these sentences. Watch for problems with word complexity, active voice, attribution, verb tense, pronouns, and phrases. If necessary, rewrite the sentences.

A PROMINENT LOCAL CLERGYMAN WAS WOUNDED IN A DRIVE-BY SHOOTING AND A WITNESS SAID HE WAS HELD AT GUNPOINT BEFORE THE INCIDENT.

———

THE EVENING NEWS REPORTED THE PLANS TO DEMOLISH A BUILDING IN THE CLARINGTON MALL WHICH IS TOO TALL FOR HEIGHT LIMITS.

———

COMPANY OFFICIALS DECLARED THEY ARE AT A LOSS TO ILLUMINATE THE ANSWER TO THE QUESTION OF THE POLLUTED AIR FROM THE DIESEL TANKS THAT COULD BE SEEN OVER THE REFINERY.

NESTED PHRASES

Another problem is the nested phrase, an interior modifying phrase that splits the parts of a sentence, usually the subject from the verb. Here's an example:

THE STORM...<u>WHICH UNTIL YESTERDAY WAS NOTHING MORE THAN A LIGHT RAINSHOWER</u>...BROUGHT HEAVY RAIN AND THUNDER TO THE KEYSTONE COUNTIES.

This type of phrase is great for prose, but lousy for broadcast narrative. Often the nested phrase is so long that the audience is hard pressed to remember what the subject was.

How do you fix a sentence with a nested phrase? One solution is to convert it into two sentences.

UNTIL YESTERDAY...THE STORM WAS NOTHING MORE THAN A LIGHT RAINSHOWER. NOW IT IS BRINGING HEAVY RAIN AND THUNDER TO THE KEYSTONE COUNTIES.

You can also fix a nested phrase by using a compound sentence.

UNTIL YESTERDAY...THE STORM WAS NOTHING MORE THAN A LIGHT RAINSHOWER...BUT NOW IT IS BRINGING HEAVY RAIN AND THUNDER TO THE KEYSTONE COUNTIES.

The use of nested phrases is an old school habit that should be reviewed by beginning broadcast writers. Always check sentences for nested phrases.

Nested Fixes

Eliminate the nested phrases from these sentences by dividing them into two sentences or forming them into compound sentences.

THE SENATE...WHICH WILL ADJOURN FOR VACATION TOMORROW AND WILL BE GONE A MONTH...WORKED LATE LAST NIGHT.

———————

THE GAS PUMPS...WHICH WERE ORIGINALLY IN THE MARINA PLANS ALONG WITH NEW PIERS AND WALKWAYS...WILL COST A MILLION DOLLARS.

———————

TEN OF THE WHALES...ON A MIGRATION FROM THE ARCTIC OCEAN TO THE WARMER WATERS OFF BAJA CALIFORNIA...BEACHED THEMSELVES YESTERDAY.

———————

THE AGENCY...BESET BY BUDGET AND STAFF MORALE PROBLEMS...FIRED 12-WORKERS THIS MORNING IN WHAT IS BEING CALLED THE MONDAY MASSACRE.

OVERLY LONG INTRODUCTORY PHRASES

There is no question that it is desirable to vary sentence structure and length. Don't do so by using long introductory phrases, however. They are useful in prose, but are to be avoided in broadcast.

This doesn't mean that introductory phrases should be eliminated altogether. You can use short (two- to four-word) phrases that convey information about time or place; however, any sentence with a long, complex opening phrase should be rewritten either as a compound sentence or as two separate ones. Here's an example of a good, short introductory phrase:

UNTIL YESTERDAY...THE LOCAL UTILITY COMPANIES COULD CHARGE WHATEVER THEY WANTED.

Here is an example of a long introductory phrase:

ALTHOUGH THE TRANSIT CARS WERE BACK ON THE TRACKS LAST THURSDAY...NO ONE IS SAYING YET HOW THE DOWNTOWN REDEVELOPMENT WILL DO.

Here's the rewrite:

THE TRANSIT CARS WERE BACK ON THE TRACKS LAST THURSDAY. NO ONE IS SAYING YET HOW THE DOWNTOWN REDEVELOPMENT IS DOING.

Here's another long intro phrase with too much information.

ALTHOUGH SEVEN SUPERVISORS VOTED AGAINST THE PROTEST GROUP'S PARADE PLANS IN THE ALL-NIGHT SESSION...THEY CLAIMED THEY WERE SYMPATHETIC.

And the rewrite, using a short time-oriented intro.

SEVEN SUPERVISORS CLAIMED THEY WERE SYMPATHETIC...BUT AT THE END OF THE ALL-NIGHT SESSION...THEY VOTED AGAINST THE PROTEST GROUP.

Working With Unneeded Introductions

In each case, decide whether the introductory phrase is too long. Edit each sentence appropriately.

ALTHOUGH IT ADDED STRENGTH TO THE NATIONAL CRACKDOWN ON DRUNK DRIVERS...THE SUPREME COURT HAS RULED POLICE CAN IGNORE A NEW LAW RESTRICTING ROADSIDE SOBRIETY TESTS.

———

ALTHOUGH FOREIGN POLICY WAS A MAJOR ISSUE SEVERAL YEARS AGO AND HAD SPARKED LOUD PROTESTS...THE STUDENTS TODAY ARE CONCERNED WITH OTHER ISSUES.

———

ALTHOUGH THE EXTRA PASSENGERS AND CAMERA EQUIPMENT STRAINED THE LIMITS OF THE HOT AIR BALLOON...THE REPORT CONCLUDED IT WAS NOT THE WEATHER THAT CAUSED IT TO FALL.

———

NOTWITHSTANDING THE NEAR RIOT AT THE RICHMOND PLANNING COMMISSION MEETING...THE PROTESTORS CONTINUED THEIR FIGHT AGAINST THE NEW AUTOMALL BALLPARK.

Comprehensive

Check these sentences for problems with active voice, complex words, attribution, verb tense, pronoun, and phrase problems. If necessary, rewrite the sentences on a separate piece of paper.

DESPITE A LAUNCH DELAY POSTPONEMENT CAUSED BY A BALKY COMPUTER...THE SPACE SHUTTLE DISCOVERY IS NOW LOCATED IN ORBIT...SAY NASA SOURCES.

———

THE TWO VICIOUS PIT BULLS...WHO NEIGHBORS SAY ALWAYS ATTACKED ANYONE IN THE VICINITY...WERE LET LOOSE BY THE POLICE.

———

ALTHOUGH THE EXPENSE TO THE STATE FOR THE RESEARCH HAD BEEN COSTLY...THE WIRE SERVICES ARE REPORTING THAT TWO UTAH DOCTORS ARE RECEIVING SPECIAL COMMENDATIONS FOR THE WORK.

———

ALTHOUGH THE WORKERS DIDN'T INTEND TO SEVER THE MULTITRUNK PHONE LINES...THE COSTLY REPAIRS MAY TAKE UNTIL FRIDAY...ACCORDING TO THE PHONE COMPANY.

REPETITION

Repetition of words and phrases is generally to be avoided. Yet, if used carefully, it can be a way of adding emphasis.

When to Avoid Repetition

Except for the verb *to say*, avoid using identical or similar verbs, nouns, and phrases in the same sentence or contiguous sentences. Here's an example.

> THE SUPREME COURT RULED TODAY THAT AN EARLIER RULING BY A FEDERAL APPEALS COURT WAS UNCONSTITUTIONAL AND THAT THE RULING SHOULD BE OVERTURNED.
> IN THAT EARLIER CASE...THE APPEALS COURT RULED FOR A MAN CONVICTED ON THE STRENGTH OF HIS CONFESSION.

Repetition often leads to confusion. It will be necessary to get rid of some of the *ruled* and *rulings*. Here's the rewrite:

> THE SUPREME COURT RULED TODAY THAT AN EARLIER DECISION BY A FEDERAL APPEALS COURT WAS UNCONSTITUTIONAL AND SHOULD BE OVERTURNED.
> IN THAT EARLIER CASE...THE APPEALS COURT REVERSED A CONVICTION INVOLVING AN ILLEGAL CONFESSION.

When to Use Repetition

Carefully planned repetition can add strength to the writing. Repeating a single word immediately after its first use adds emphasis. This is an example of a sentence without emphasis:

> THE CITY COUNCIL TODAY PASSED A LAW THAT WILL END SPECULATION IN HOUSING IN PORTLAND.

But if you repeat the word *law*, it gains emphasis:

> THE CITY COUNCIL TODAY PASSED A LAW...A LAW THAT WILL END SPECULATION IN HOUSING IN PORTLAND.

Avoiding Common Repetition

Edit these sentences to eliminate repetition.

THEY ARE PLANNING TO USE THE DOWNTOWN PLAN AS A GUIDE FOR FUTURE PLANNING IN THE DISTRICT.

———————

THEY'RE NOWHERE NEAR THEIR GOAL OF GETTING THE MONEY THERE TO THE HOSPITAL.

———————

THE DIVISION OF FORESTRY IS SOUNDING THE ALARM ABOUT AN ALARMING FUNGUS BLIGHT EATING AWAY AT THE PINE FORESTS OF GEORGIA.

———————

CAR DEALERS ALONG THE PARKWAY WILL HAVE TO COVER THEIR CARS WHEN THE PAVING BEGINS NEXT WEEK.

Repetition for Emphasis

In each sentence, use repetition to emphasize the underlined word.

BIGTOWN STEEL EMPLOYEES ARE SETTING A <u>GOAL</u> TO PRODUCE MORE THAN LAST YEAR'S OUTPUT.

———————

THE JURY RETURNED A GUILTY <u>VERDICT</u>. IT IS A DANGEROUS ACT BECAUSE OF THREATS DURING THE TRIAL.

Now, you choose a word, either a noun or an adjective, to emphasize by repetition.

THE WARSHIP MADE AN EMOTIONAL HOMECOMING. IT HAD BEEN AT SEA FOR 14-MONTHS.

———————

THE MAYOR SAID THE BUDGET DEFICIT WAS SIGNIFICANT BECAUSE THE CITY HAD NO WAY TO GET THE MONEY.

———————

THE TRIAL JUDGE WARNED THE DECISION WOULD MAKE A LOT OF PEOPLE ANGRY BECAUSE MANY HAD HOPED THE SENIOR CITIZEN COULD KEEP HER HOME.

CHAPTER SUMMARY

This chapter provides some guidelines that will help you write effectively for broadcast. Keep the following points in mind:

- Use short, active words.
- Write elliptical sentences to mimic speech patterns.
- Attribution goes first.
- Choose active voice always.
- Use participial verb forms.
- Avoid ambiguous pronouns.
- Watch for out-of-place phrases.
- Avoid long introductory and nested phrases.
- Remember that carefully planned repetition of words can add strength to your writing.

It goes without saying that all of these rules can be broken when it is appropriate to do so; however, following these guidelines is a major step in learning to develop a writing style that will work well in broadcast.

4

Writing the Compelling Lead

CHAPTER PREVIEW

Broadcast lead sentences must not only serve the same function as newspaper headlines and story leads, but also be the starting point of a carefully constructed narrative account. In major stories, the lead is usually obvious, but in minor stories, writers must look to keywords and use devices such as irony, common wisdom, or the unexpected. Often, you can determine what should go into the lead by examining what in the story affects you, the writer. This chapter looks at various categories of leads: new story; reaction (reax); update, second-day, or follow-up (folo); perspective; segues; and soft or feature leads. It also examines what to avoid, including jammed, cliché, question, and quote leads.

GLOSSARY

BREAKING NEWS   An unexpected event that requires consideration of coverage.

CLICHÉ LEAD   A type of lead sentence that is built around an overused phrase.

COMMON WISDOM   A generally accepted account of something, usually without scientific proof.

EXCEPTION LEAD   A lead sentence that focuses on an unexpected event.

FEATURE OR SOFT LEAD   A lead sentence often used when the story angle does not involve timely or deadline information. This type of lead is usually long, and is usually constructed of information not found in the story.

FOLO LEAD   (for follow up) A lead sentence that advances the information of a new or breaking story. Same as the update or second-day lead.

IMMEDIACY CUE   Word or phrase that adds a heightened sense of time to a story. Examples would be "This just in" or "At this moment."

IRONY   A narrative device that focuses on the opposite of the expected result or meaning.

JAMMED LEAD   A lead sentence that attempts to include all story facts. Jammed leads should be avoided.

KEYWORDS   Items in a story that trigger interest in themes, perspective, events, or details.

PERSPECTIVE LEAD   A lead sentence that relates the current story to previous events or trends.

QUESTION LEAD   A lead sentence that begins with a rhetorical question. It is to be avoided.

QUOTE LEAD   A lead sentence that begins with an unattributed quote. It is to be avoided.

REAX LEAD   (for reaction) A lead that emphasizes the responses of persons or groups to previous stories.

SECOND-DAY LEAD   This is the first attempt to restructure the information from a breaking story. It could happen on the second day. Also called the *folo*.

SEGUE   A transition between parts of a presentation. In news, the segue is the the transition into the next story. A segue lead ties a story to the preceding story.

LEADS

When writing for broadcast, you should be spending a good portion of your time puzzling over the lead and how it will be written. The function of the lead in broadcast is far more complex and critical than it is in a newspaper.

The newspaper has a headline, written by the copyeditor, which is there to attract the eye of the reader, and a lead written by the reporter, which is the beginning of a story to which the reader has already been drawn. In the newspaper, the headline attracts and the lead simply kicks off the story.

But in broadcast, the lead must do both jobs. It must draw the audience to the story topic, while beginning the flow of information. For this reason, it is crucial that the broadcast lead be clever, tight, attractive, and informative.

A second reason for a good broadcast lead is the audience's wavering attention. The radio may be in the car and the television somewhere across the room. As we mentioned in Chapter 1, the audiences may be doing other things while listening to or watching the news. You have to break into their conversations and get their attention to interest them in the story.

TRADITIONAL NEWS VALUES

Some stories are going to be interesting and attract viewers no matter what's in the lead. These are the major stories—big ones in anyone's book—and you'll have to mess these up to keep people from watching. On a good day, you might have three or four major stories.

On a bad news day, there may not be any major stories; in fact, you may be dealing with stories that fall into the next category—medium-interest stories, or second-tier stories. To identify what's interesting, look for something in these categories:

- *Effect on the viewers.* People are very interested if their money, jobs, personal security, or family are threatened. This is known by some as "heart, health, and pocketbook."

- *Proximity.* Viewers and listeners like stories that involve people or things close to them, such as the neighborhood, the city, relatives or friends, or their friends' neighborhoods and cities.

- *Prominence.* Prominence includes stories about highly visible personalities such as entertainment stars, religious leaders, or politicians. Also, any stories about national or international governmental actions at a high level, actions in the area of social order such as war, or social events or themes that carry an importance solely by definition, such as health, education, or science

- *Human interest.* People enjoy stories about successes, failures, and curious events of unknown people, as well as stories about common, everyday happenings in life.

WHAT INTERESTS ME ABOUT THIS STORY?

If it isn't immediately obvious which category the medium-interest story is in, trust your own judgment. Read the wire copy or your notes and underline words that carry the story's theme. These are keywords. Then look at what you underlined. It answers the question, What interests me about this story? Was it new details, the tragedy, the success, the bold plan, the risk taken, the irony, or the failure? Did someone fight city hall or rise from obscurity? If you can isolate an answer, you'll have the topic area for your lead. Your own sense of news must become the yardstick.

Here's an example of some story notes with keywords underlined.

Re: Dolphins and theories of communication

From: Researchers at the Saltmarsh Sea Mammal Park

Scientists now believe <u>dolphins communicate</u> for playful as well as <u>serious reasons</u>. In the past, researchers thought that the mammals only used their <u>underwater squeaks and whistles</u> to <u>warn of danger</u> or suggest food availability. Now...the new research at Saltmarsh seems to indicate that dolphins <u>play games to pass the time</u> at sea. The research was done over a <u>seven-year period</u> and was led by Dr. Bivalve Watson.

Once you've underlined the keywords, you've got some idea of what has triggered your interest. As an example, in the fifth line, the keywords "playful events" are underlined. They could be the focus in your lead.

HOW MUCH OF THE STORY GOES INTO THE LEAD?

Very little, is the answer. Broadcast leads are best when they are short and have only enough information to suggest the guts of the story. Attempt to answer one of two questions in the lead—where and what? Or where, and what is the intensity of the story? The *where* is easy, but the *what* or intensity is more complex.

Underlined keywords help define the *what*. The *what* should not be too general, or it could just as well lead to a different story and will lack appeal. Here's a general lead, accurate but uninteresting.

> SCIENTISTS AT THE SALTMARSH SEA PARK HAVE SOME NEW RE-SEARCH ABOUT DOLPHINS.

This is much too general and not very exciting. You don't see many keywords replayed here. With this lead, you might only be cueing a segment of the audience who were generally interested in whether the researchers are still alive.

Don't ignore your keywords. Say the "playful events" element intrigued you. Put that in or near the lead. To reach an audience more interested in the general concepts of the story, the lead must be more precise. Here's your rewrite.

> FOR YEARS SCIENTISTS THOUGHT DOLPHINS MADE UNDERWATER SOUNDS ONLY TO WARN OTHER DOLPHINS ABOUT DANGER.
> NOW SOME NEW RESEARCH SAYS THE DOLPHINS ALSO COMMUNICATE FOR SOCIAL REASONS...SUCH AS PLAYING GAMES.

That's better. More elements that intrigued you are in this lead or its next sentence. It attracts not only people generally interested in marine biology, but also those who are fascinated by our relationship with other creatures on the planet and with attempts to communicate with them.

AVOID HYPE IN LEADS

A television station in a major California market once had an unwritten but well-known policy that urged its newswriters to insert adjectives such as *bizarre*, *stunning*, *spectacular*, or *one-of-a-kind* into almost every lead. The stories all sounded like this:

THE CITY COUNCIL...IN A STUNNING MOVE...IS GOING TO...

The constant use of such words crosses the line into hype or sensationalism, which is the repeated use of certain elements to thrill or amaze. At some point, it must have desensitized the audience.

If you have stories that are indeed bizarre, you don't need to hype them. Your audience will catch on if your lead gives away enough of the story.

CATEGORIES OF LEADS

There are many different approaches to writing leads. Although it is difficult to group leads into categories, we will consider those which occur most often: new story, reax, update or second-day, perspective, exception, segue, and feature leads. There are other ways to set up valid categories, but for the purpose of our exercises we will use these.

New Story (Breaking News) Leads

New story leads are the normal, everyday variety that are used for unexpected, breaking items. This could be a sudden event, a scientific report, a crime story, or any action on a new topic. Whatever the theme, the new story lead is the first time that the audience will hear about this story.

Newspaper style allows you to summarize the entire story in the lead sentence, but for radio and television you must learn to hold back some of the information in a new story lead. Broadcast stories spread out the information, releasing a little at a time. The leads have only a few details, generally the *what* and the *where*. The *who* and the *why* come later. The *when* will either be highlighted or ignored.

Including only a few details in a new story lead is generally enough to hold the audience's interest. Here's an example of the *what* and the *where* in a lead.

A MAN DROVE HIS CAR THROUGH A DOWNTOWN STEELTOWN BANK WINDOW.

In this lead, the writer is offering a few facts, but saving the identification (who) for later and the reason (why) for the central part of the story.

New story leads will be possible in fewer than 25 percent of your stories, but because the goal is to release only a few details, the new leads often are the toughest to write. Try keeping the word count in the lead to 11 words or under.

Writing New Story Leads

Write a lead for both of these situations.

Situation 1

You are writing for the 8 a.m. morning newscast.

You get a handout from the Steeltown Transit District saying they are planning to spend $2,243,000 to redesign and rebuild some of the new articulated buses they recently purchased.

The work will start in one month.

Until the overhauls, though, more and more of the new buses will be out of service because they cannot be fixed. That leaves the district short on running stock and unable to make all the runs. Service for many commuters to downtown and back will be curtailed, meaning delays of up to 30 minutes on some lines.

With a few calls, you learn that the work is being done because of a Transit District mistake in ordering the buses. The wrong gears were selected and the wear and tear on the ones chosen has destroyed many of the transmissions.

Write your lead here:

Situation 2

At their regular Tuesday meeting, the board of supervisors heard a report about a toxic substance on the tile surfaces of the McDermott Park public swimming pool. Health Director Shirley McClean suggested draining the pool and having it scrubbed. The supervisors debated this, because summer break has started and the pool is busy every day. The county attorney told the supervisors they would be liable if anyone became ill from the substance. Supervisors voted 7-0 to close the pool for one week.

Write your lead here:

Reax Leads

This is a good lead for any story more than four hours but generally less than a day old. Basically, a reax lead advances the story, concentrating on the reaction of someone who comments on the initial event. To find that person, ask Who will be affected? Get a response from that person and it becomes the lead. Then you can follow with information about the initial event.

An example would be the city manager's action to fire the transit district director. Even if that was done at a late-night meeting and you are uncertain whether your audience has heard about it or read it in the paper, your broadcast lead the next morning might not be the firing as much as the reaction (reax) to the firing. It's both an update and an advance to the story. Here's the reax lead on that one.

SOME OF STEELTOWN'S BUS DRIVERS SAY THEY ARE UNHAPPY THEIR BOSS WAS FIRED LAST NIGHT...

The next paragraph explains what happened; then in the fourth or fifth paragraph, return to the reaction. The reax lead is a good choice, because of the need to advance the information.

A word of caution. Don't overuse "immediacy cues," words that tell the audience what hot stuff this story is. Because the time element is so crucial in the reax or second-day lead, it is necessary to exercise restraint in beating the audience over the head concerning your news-gathering abilities. Be careful when even minor stories get the following kind of treatment.

REACTION TO THE SUDDEN TRANSIT FIRING IS STARTLING THIS MORNING <u>AND YOU ARE HEARING IT FIRST NOW</u>.
SOME OF THE DISGRUNTLED BUS DRIVERS ARE TELLING K-560 NEWS EXCLUSIVELY THAT THEY ARE UNHAPPY THEIR BOSS GOT HIS PINK SLIP...AND THAT HE HAD BEEN DOING A GREAT JOB GETTING THE SYSTEM BACK ON TRACK.

Reax Leads

Review each situation and write a reax lead. Keep your leads under 11 words.

SAMPLE: Situation A

For a 6 p.m. newscast. The president, a Republican, at 10 a.m. accuses the Democrats of undermining a proposed law that would assist veterans who are looking for mortgages to buy houses.

At 4 p.m., the Democratic House leader responds, saying the it was the Republicans who stalled the bill because of a rider that would have allowed more school financing.

EXAMPLE:

CONGRESSIONAL DEMOCRATS ARE SAYING THEY AREN'T THE ONES WHO STOPPED THE NEW VETERANS HOME BUYING BILL.

Situation B

For the 11 p.m. newscast. You have the White House announcement (5 p.m.) that U.S. troops will go to the Balkans on a peace-keeping mission. At 7:30 p.m., Democrats respond that the president never consulted Congress and they will stop the orders.

Write your lead for B here:

Situation C

For the 8 a.m. news cut-in in the morning. At 8 p.m. last evening, a critic of the mayor announced that the FBI is investigating the contracts awarded for the new airport terminal. It made the late newscasts and the morning paper. At 6:30 this morning, the mayor, interviewed on a local talk-radio show, says this is false. The mayor says there is no investigation.

Write your lead for C here:

Second-Day, Folo, or Update Leads

A second-day, folo, or update lead advances an earlier story. These leads are looking for the next step in the story, whether it be an investigation, explanation, action taken by government, or whatever. These differ from the reax because these are not based on a personal reaction to the story.

Although the update, second-day, and folo leads are essentially the same, there is a slight difference. The update can come at any time. The second-day lead is usually the beginning of the major newscast the next day. A folo lead can update, or it can branch off to a sidebar.

These types of leads present the problem of estimating how much background the public remembers and how much is needed to brief them. If your lead is this,

AN APPEALS COURT HAS REVERSED AN IMPORTANT RULING IN THE FLORIDA ELECTION CASE.

your listeners or viewers may not remember which court decision you are talking about. A better update lead reveals a topic to the ruling:

AN APPEALS COURT HAS REVERSED A FLORIDA ORDER TO RECOUNT DAMAGED BALLOTS IN SEMINOLE COUNTY.

Second-Day, Folios, or Updates

Review these examples of wire service copy. Note in each that there are events that took place yesterday and events that are more recent. Be sure to focus on the most recent events for your lead. Now write the lead sentence of each story. Keep your lead to 11 words.

BERNOULLI, France (PL)...A 270 foot unsinkable ferryboat capsized and sank yesterday in choppy seas in the mouth of the harbor at Ostende, Belgium.

All 37 passengers and the crew of six were rescued, officials said late last night. The ferryboat had just completed a trip from Dover, England, and now is resting on its side in only 40 feet of water. It is a hazard to navigation, authorities conceded. At this point, officials are closing the Ostende harbor until they decide what to do about the sunken ferryboat.

Write your lead here:

ASHRAM, India (PL)...The Indian government is not looking kindly on the return of the controversial American guru Abba and his followers.

According to today's reports in New Delhi papers, the government has issued orders to make his stay in India as difficult as possible. Yesterday, the guru and four members of his party had to secure special travel permits for moving around within India. Also, the guru must travel by bus after his special car permits were denied. The Indian government has assigned agents to travel with him.

The U.S. government is interested in the guru's travels. He is wanted in the U.S. on felony charges for gun possession and illegal land possession.

Write your lead here:

Perspective Leads

Perspective is overview—a comparison with current situations, the past, or other associated material—and it is the journalist's job to provide perspective if needed for each story. In newspapers that may come several paragraphs after the lead, but in broadcast it's more common to find perspective in the lead, because a perspective lead most closely resembles the opening of a conversation, in which a person might say "Well, it's happened again."

Quite often the perspective on the story is what makes it interesting; by placing perspective in the lead, you are alerting the audience right away to the most intriguing element. So to write a perspective lead, you ignore the immediacy, the new reax, or the update on the item. Instead, you begin with the overview—how this event fits into the pattern. To find the perspective, ask yourself:

1. *Is this story related to current controversies or other events?* For example, even if you have new information about one of many buildings burned in today's flash brush fire, your lead might ignore it. Instead, the lead will wrap various damage reports together, giving a perspective on the growing tragedy.

    FIRE OFFICIALS ARE NOW SAYING THE ROGERS FLAT FIRE IS THE BIGGEST IN TEN YEARS.

2. *Does this topic fit into any historical pattern?* For example, if this story is about a monkey that has escaped from the local zoo, and you know there have been a number of escapes, then you might want to bypass the new story lead and go instead with the perspective lead. Here's an example of how not to write your lead:

    A MONKEY ESCAPED FROM THE STEELTOWN ZOO THIS MORNING

    This is usable but dull because it doesn't have perspective. A perspective lead relates today's event to a pattern:

    FOR THE THIRD TIME THIS MONTH...A MONKEY IS ON THE LOOSE   TONIGHT.
    IT ESCAPED FROM THE ZOO'S MONKEY ISLAND EXHIBIT SOME-TIME THIS MORNING.
    ZOOKEEPERS THINK...

Perspective leads are very popular and you'll be writing a lot of them. Only one word of caution. Do not add perspective if you haven't researched the facts or don't understand the situation. A cardinal rule of journalism, "Don't assume anything," is never more important than here. Check your facts carefully.

EXERCISE 4-D

Perspective Leads

Review the situation notes, mark keywords, and write the first :15 of each story. Your leads should be no more than 11 words long.

Situation 1

Three days of torrential rain. Serious flooding now. These are reports from the suburbs of Steeltown.

In Carrington Falls, a canyon flooded and two houses were completely lost. No injuries. In East Merimac, a drainage culvert backed up and millions of gallons of runoff flooded the Eastvale Shopping Center. Water is thee feet deep. No injuries, but 24 stores affected and millions in damage. In Bestwicke, a house slid down a hillside, and crumbled the back wall of a cookie store on the street below. No one was hurt.

Write your lead here:

Situation 2

No negotiations today and none scheduled tomorrow. This is now the 45th day of the first hospital workers strike in Brayer County in 10 years. Local 231 of the Hospital Workers wants a 4 percent raise, but the county says it cannot pay any raises this year. There are 600 workers out at four locations. Only doctors are working at the hospitals, and only emergency services are offered.

Write your lead here:

Exception or Irony Leads

While there is no rhyme or reason that this should have its own category, exception or irony is used so often that it stands out.

The exception lead uses the one-of-a-kind nature of the situation as the lead. All you need to ask is: Is this unusual or somehow outside of the normal way things happen?

For instance, a zoo shuttle bus driver on her first day makes a wrong turn and ends up at a nearby shopping center where the driver has to call for help. The lead may sound like this:

NORMALLY...THE ELEPHANT TRAIN AT THE ZOO TAKES YOU TO THE ANIMALS...BUT TODAY WAS DIFFERENT.

Or take this touching account:

DEPUTY SHERIFF LANCE BEAME WAS STANDING BESIDE A SOFT DRINK MACHINE WHEN HE HEARD IT MEOW...AND THAT'S HOW THE LITTLE LOST KITTEN BOOTSY WAS FOUND.

Irony leads note when something is exactly the opposite of what is expected.

NORMALLY...PIGS LIVE OUTSIDE...BUT IN MAR VISTA ESTATES... LUANN MELTON HAS GIVEN KITCHEN ACCESS RIGHTS TO HER POT-BELLIED PIG.

Exception or Irony Leads

Write exception or irony leads for the following situations. Keep each lead to 11 words or less. Work on a separate sheet of paper.

1. A gambling barge, which normally is tied up on the Mississippi side of the river, where gambling is legal, broke loose and ended up in an Arkansas county, where gambling is illegal.

2. A feeder airline pilot became confused while on approach to Ft. Lauderdale and landed at the wrong airport.

3. A bank mistakenly direct-deposits extra money in a retired man's account. When he went looking for his usual $1,500, he had $1,500,000.

4. Swallows usually nest in the recesses of roof eaves around the city, but this year one bird happily set up a nest in a streetlight that hangs over one of the major intersections.

5. City gardeners, who usually ride on large, gas-powered mowers to cut the grass, this year have brought in a herd of goats.

6. Benjamin Ellsberg found a machine gear in a bowl of breakfast cereal, the same cereal he has eaten for the past 25 years.

7. A mother dog has adopted a stray kitten as part of its litter.

8. A group of seniors from the Westfield Retirement Home went skydiving. Everyone who participated was over 75.

9. A car thief tried to steal an unmarked patrol car while the undercover deputies were outside it making a phone call.

Segue Leads

Segue is a music term describing the interval between songs. It is used as a noun to describe a transition ("a tight segue") or as a verb ("to segue from X to Y"). In news, the term describes the transition from one story to the next.

A segue lead for story B is based on key themes in story A. The producer makes this happen by clustering similar stories in the newscast. Once the story rundown is locked in, it's possible to write a segue lead where contiguous stories have the same themes.

Sometimes the segues are easy and are natural flows from the previous story. But often you may have to look hard for keywords in story A to make that leap to story B. The segue lead can be based on story conditions, as well as on time or location.

Segues From Story Conditions.   Say, the previous story, story A, is about an escaped rhesus monkey. The story that follows, story B, for which you are writing a segue lead, is about the arrival of new pandas at the zoo.

> ZOOKEEPERS HAD A MUCH MORE PLEASANT EXPERIENCE TODAY WHEN TWO RARE PANDAS...

This lead allows story B to roll from the information in story A. But suppose your editor wants the segue to be related in a different way. Story A is still the zoo story, but story B is about a prison escape. It might be far-fetched, but that depends upon how you handle it. Here's an example of a segue lead for story B.

> AN ESCAPE OF A DIFFERENT NATURE...AND FAR MORE DANGEROUS...AT COUNTY JAIL...

Geographic or Time Segues.   These are most common and are often added later by a newscaster. Here's a geographic example for the prison escape.

> ALSO IN BRAYER COUNTY...TWO MEN WHO...

A geographic or time segue is certainly not as clever or thoughtful as the others, and should be saved for the last-minute when brainpower has failed for the day.

The Dangers of Segue Leads.   The segue lead's biggest trap is the attempt to make a connection that isn't there. That's happened too many times in news. A second problem arises when the producer drops story A from the newscast, leaving story B with a lead that doesn't make sense.

Say the first story is about new federal regulations allowing retirees to access more of their IRA savings accounts, and the second story is about a conservation group who cleaned up a creekbed to save it from erosion. So the writer develops a segue lead.

> AND A DIFFERENT KIND OF SAVING WENT ON TODAY AT CACHE CREEK WHEN...

As you can see, if the IRA story gets dropped that segue wouldn't work.

Segue Leads

Review the situations and write segue leads for stories 2 and 3 based on the stories that precede them. Your leads should be no more than 11 words long.

Story 1

COMMUTERRAIL WILL BE SLOWING DOWN THE MORNING TRAIN SERVICE FROM MAR VISTA ESTATES TO STEELTOWN.

TRANSIT OFFICIALS SAY THE SPEED REDUCTIONS ARE NEEDED BECAUSE THEY WILL BE REPAIRING THE TRACKS.

THEY ESTIMATE THE SLOWER TRAINS WILL ONLY ADD 10 MINUTES TO THE COMMUTE.

Situation for Story 2

CommuterRail train drivers will begin a job action on Monday...because they have been working without a contract for the past three months. They will follow all safety rules and won't work overtime.

Write a segue lead here for Story 2.

Situation for Story 3

Worldwide Airlines will open its new corporate offices in downtown Steeltown Monday. The 4,000 employees who will begin work that day used to work in Mar Vista headquarters. It is expected many will depend on CommuterRail trains to get to work.

Write a segue lead here for Story 3.

Feature or Soft Leads

Many times you will work on a story that is timeless and can be held for weeks without getting old. Often called an *evergreen* or an *H-F-R* (for hold for release), this type of feature fits in the area of soft news—the human interest feature story. These stories don't have the angle of immediacy, or reax, or perspective. In many cases, it will take a clever bit of writing to fashion the lead.

The lead for the feature story can often be found in the more universal themes it represents or in the commonsense lesson it provides. In unusual cases, you might have to resort to well-known quotations, sayings, metaphors, song lyrics, or poems.

Let's say this story involves a construction worker who has invented a special drill for the new Steeltown sewer project. It's not a new story, or a reax, or a folo. There's not a lot of perspective to use. Certainly, there's no segue in sight.

The feature lead is what's left. Here, the writer has chosen to highlight the unusual nature of this event.

> MOST WORKERS COME TO THE JOB...PUT IN EIGHT HOURS...AND HEAD HOME.
> BUT SOME ARE LOOKING FOR WAYS TO IMPROVE WHAT THEY DO.
> ONE OF THOSE IS STEELTOWN SEWER WORKS WELDER AURELIO CASTENAGA.
> WHILE WORKING ON...

Problems With Feature Leads. Backing into the story with a feature lead can be dangerous at times because the lead can grow to unwieldy lengths, often more than half of the time allotted for the story. It took, for instance, almost :10 to get into the drill invention story example. That might have gone even longer.

A second danger of feature leads is that the theme of the metaphor, quotation, or joke may not fit the situation. Here's an example of that problem:

> THOMAS EDISON ONCE SAID INVENTORS ARE CRAZY PEOPLE...BENT ON SAVING THE WORLD BY TINKERING.
> AND THAT'S WHAT ONE SEWER WORKER HAS BEEN DOING LATELY... GOING CRAZY IN THE PIPELINES...BECAUSE HE DIDN'T HAVE A DURABLE BIT FOR HIS DRILL...

That one might even draw a lawsuit. It also emphasizes the third danger of the feature lead—inaccuracy of the chosen quote, saying, or whatever is used. For instance, did Thomas Edison really say that? Look it up. Maybe the reporter only half-remembers the famous old saying. If you don't, there are hundreds of viewers out there who know it exactly, and they probably won't be timid about calling in to let the staff know about the mistake.

Feature Leads

Review the situation notes, circle the keywords, and write two different :15 feature leads for this story, one using an old saying or proverb, and the other using a feature lead of your choice.

Situation

Two men are attempting to break the tandem bicycle record across the United States. They will leave tomorrow from a downtown San Francisco park and head east to the boardwalk in Atlantic City. They are Michael Denton, 37, of Arlington, Virginia, and William Popper, 24, of Devonshire Springs, Maryland. They are doing this to raise money for the Muscular Dystrophy Fund. The attempt is unusual because Popper is blind. They will be followed by a van carrying spare parts and personal belongings. They expect the trip will take 18 days.

Write both leads here:

LEADS TO AVOID

Some leads are awkward. Although not grammatically wrong, they can put the newscaster in a difficult situation with long sentences, dull writing, or questionable emphasis on words. The four we will consider are the jammed, cliché, question, and quote leads. None of these is forever banished; rather, they should be used sparingly, if at all.

Avoid Jammed Leads

A jammed lead is similar to the newspaper inverted pyramid lead, in which the writer attempts to tell the entire story in one sentence. In broadcast, it just doesn't work. Both the broadcaster and the audience need the pauses provided by scripts designed for speech patterns.

The best method of fixing a jammed lead is to break it up into a number of sentences or to focus on some keywords in the story and try for a new story or perspective lead.

Here's a jammed lead.

ON A VOTE OF FIVE-TO-TWO...THE SANTA CLARA SUPERVISORS ARE PUTTING ON HOLD TWO MULTI-MILLION DOLLAR SEWER PROJECTS UNTIL A SUPERVISORS COMMITTEE BEGINS TO INVESTIGATE THE CHARGES OF FRAUD...MISMANAGEMENT...AND POLITICAL FAVORITISM IN THE AWARD OF THE LUCRATIVE CONTRACTS FOR THE WORK ON THE NEW TREATMENT PLANT INGRESS PIPES.

Here's the rewrite:

SANTA CLARA SUPERVISORS ARE PUTTING TWO EXPENSIVE SEWER PROJECTS ON HOLD.

(((EXERCISE 4-H)))

Avoid Jammed Leads

Review the situation notes, underline some keywords, and write a :15 lead for this story. Keep the word count under 11.

Situation

You're working on the 6 p.m. news. At 3:00 this afternoon, a runaway truck smashed into a house under construction on a hillside above an elementary school in the Walnut Vista section of Steeltown. The truck tore the half-finished house from its foundation, and the truck and house plunged into the schoolyard. The house was worth $225,000, the truck was worth $15,000, and the load of glass the truck was carrying was worth $10,000. Two teenagers were playing basketball in the otherwise empty schoolyard. They pulled the driver, Roger Barnes, 36, out of the cab. Barnes was later arrested by city police for drunken driving and taken to jail.

Write your lead here:

Avoid Cliché Leads

Although clichés are easy to insert for leads, they should be avoided and an effort made to write a more clever opening.

The most overused cliché leads are the "good news/bad news" ones that seem to pop up in almost every newscast.

> THERE'S GOOD NEWS FOR CAR BUYERS...

or

> BAD NEWS FOR TAXPAYERS. THE...

or

> THERE'S GOOD NEWS AND BAD NEWS FOR DOG LOVERS...

The difficulty with "good news/bad news" leads or any other cliché is overuse. Because different writers prepare a single broadcast, the "good news/bad news" leads can show up twice or three times in a newscast. When this happens, the leads lack punch. Also, a "good news" lead is a bit of editorializing on our part. Maybe it was good news for some, but it could have been bad news for others.

Practice writing all of your stories without using "good news" or "bad news" leads. The day will come when you are overloaded with work, the deadline is five minutes away, and your brain has ceased to function. That's the time to resurrect this tired old lead.

Avoid Question Leads

Question leads are an old broadcast standby. They show up in plenty of newscasts—more than they need to. As with cliché leads, the question format becomes stale after the second or third use.

> WHAT IS RED AND WHITE AND GREEN ALL OVER? WELL...IT ISN'T THE ZEBRA AT THE ZOO BECAUSE...

or

> WHAT DOES EVERYONE DOWN AT COUNTY JAIL WANT IN THE OLD CHRISTMAS STOCKING?
> WELL...IT COULD BE A GOOD PAIR OF EAR PLUGS...

For now, avoid using questions for leads. As you become more skilled, and are writing for yourself, there's nothing wrong with occasionally using this opening.

There is another point to consider. Questions are tough on the newscaster, especially if he or she is someone other than the writer and is surprised by the question. Sometimes it's hard to get the right inflection. Other times, the question may simply allow the audience to answer "no" or "so what" and then ignore your story.

((• **EXERCISE 4-1** •))

Turning Around the Question

Follow the example and change the question leads.

WHAT IS THE BEST WAY TO COMMUTE TO WORK?
ALMOST ANYONE WHO RIDES THE BUS WILL TELL YOU
THAT...

To change this example, eliminate the question and start with the answer.

ALMOST EVERYONE WHO RIDES THE BUS WOULD TELL YOU
THAT...

Now turn around these question leads:

WHO IS THE LUCKIEST POLITICIAN THIS YEAR?
IT MIGHT HAVE BEEN BOB BOSTWICK...THE NEW STATE
CONTROLLER.

WHAT'S THE MOST DANGEROUS INTERSECTION IN THE
CITY? WELL...A NEW STUDY SAYS IT'S THE CORNER OF B
AND OAK STREETS.

Write your leads here:

Avoid Unnecessary Quotes as Leads

Cold quotes, which are quotes without advance attribution, are tempting. They are dramatic. They sometimes stun the listeners and viewers. Sometimes, they even work—maybe once a month.

In the meantime, don't use unattributed quotes as leads. Otherwise you put your newscasters in jeopardy. Quotes need dramatic reading, and most newscasters are not ready to adopt a persona at the top of every story. In the next example, an unattributed quote appeared in a newscast after a story about an unexpected tragedy. This was the lead.

> I AM SADDENED...DISMAYED...AND SICKENED BY THIS WHOLE MESS.
> THOSE WERE THE WORDS TODAY OF...

Unfortunately, it was easy to confuse the opening quote with the end of the previous story. In this case, the newscaster realized what had happened and she became flustered during the remainder of the story. Before a quote, put in advance attribution.

EXERCISE 4-J

Leads

Review the situation, underline the keywords, and write two leads for this story.

Situation

This occurred at Hilltop Metropolitan hospital last night at 11:30 p.m. A neighborhood power failure had knocked out electricity to various parts of the hospital. Emergency generators kicked in everywhere except for one operating room, in which a Cesarean section birth was underway.

A quick-thinking nurse grabbed a flashlight from another room and held it for doctors while they continued the operation. The lights were restored in 10 minutes and everything went okay. Chief surgeon Dr. Mary Wentz said it certainly made for an interesting operation. The baby girl, named Luz (for light), is fine. Her mother, Maria Espinoza, 24, of Steeltown, said she is thrilled by the nurse's quick thinking. The nurse, Byron Walcott, 28, Fairview, said it was his camping flashlight and he was lucky he was just back from a trip. "When I turned it on," he said, "I hoped I had remembered to put in new batteries. It was weak, but by some miracle, it kept on long enough."

Write your leads here:

More Leads

Review the situation, underline the keywords, and write two leads for this story.

Situation

The school board met last night, and after a routine 5-hour session, they voted to close five elementary schools, all in the Riverview district, which has a high minority population. The board says the closures will save over $2 million in the next three years. The students from the closed schools will be bused to schools in Manor Heights, which is a very rich suburb, with few minority residents.

At the meeting, parents from Riverview charged racism was involved in the reassignments. They pointed out that the schools were closed in their district because all of the school board members and the superintendent live in Manor Heights. You are unable to confirm whether or not that is true. However, you do learn it will cost over $1.5 million for the busing program in three years, an expense the district wouldn't have without the closures.

Write your leads here:

CHAPTER SUMMARY

The writer has an important job in preparing the lead for a broadcast story. On radio and television, the lead sentence substitutes for both the headline and story lead in print. It must draw attention while starting the story.

Writers might be able to build leads around the story's effect on the viewer, proximity, prominence of those involved, and the human-interest angle. Many categories of leads are available, including new story, reax, second-day/update, perspective, exception, segue, and feature. Writers should avoid jamming too much information into the lead, or beginning stories with clichés, quotes, or questions.

5

Getting Interviews:
The Powerful Soundbite

CHAPTER PREVIEW

This chapter covers the unique nature of recorded field interviews and shows how the inclusion of a portion of one of these—a bite, or soundbite—dramatically changes the simple rules of read-only scripts.

A broadcast journalist must constantly switch back and forth between two types of interviews: those done for research and those done to become potent segments of stories. The recorded interview is seeking (a) eyewitness accounts, (b) competent professional evaluation, (c) informed response to charges, or (d) the effect of a trend or event on the interviewee. Before an interview, a journalist should be thinking about asking *how* and *why* questions and avoiding questions that lead to mere *yes* and *no* answers.

Most interview bites will influence the construction of the story, from the lead to the tag. In this book, the sentence immediately before the bite will be called the *writeup,* and there are definite rules about its design.

GLOSSARY

AMBIENT SOUND   Recorded sound that is not part of an interview. It is also called *NAT sound* (for natural sound), *wild sound, background,* or *BG sound.*

BITE   The recorded interview portion that has been pulled for use in a news story. Also called a *cut.*

EXPERT SOURCE   A contact or person whose experience or professional knowledge will allow them to speak competently about a topic.

VOX POP   The shortened version of *vox populi,* or voice of the people. Vox pop has also been called "man on the street."

WRITEUP   The broadcast story sentence immediately preceding a bite. It is also called the *lead-in,* the *intro,* the *throw line,* or the *ID.*

ACTUALITIES AND SOUNDBITES

Soundbites, like used car dealers, have a bad reputation. With each political campaign, critics zero in on the "soundbite" as if it were some newly discovered evil of nature. But soundbites are simply the broadcast equivalent of quotes—something used by print writers since the first newsbooks in the 16th century.

When a soundbite (radio or television) is introduced into a story, the bite contributes strength. Bites provide more than the simple spoken text in the quote; often viewers and listeners glean just as much from the nature of the delivery, the body language, gestures, and emotion of the situation, as well as the ambient background sounds. At times, these secondary subtextual elements carry as much information as what is said and could, in some situations, even contradict the meaning in the spoken text.

The test for using a soundbite is simple—its combination of the information in the bite's words and the body language, gestures, and emotion revealed by the speaker must provide the viewer and listener with more than the newswriter could possibly craft into a script. Simply put, if the interviewee merely recites a laundry list of facts about the operation, you don't need the bite. You can write that. But if the interviewee emotionally tells why the operation is so valuable, then the bite is probably more powerful than your script. That's when you use the bite.

INTERVIEWS NEED PLANNING

Securing a strong soundbite or actuality means extra thought must go into planning the interview. Good actualities seldom just happen; they are the product of careful preparation.

The first move is to shrewdly select the interviewee. Assume a new assignment editor suggests that you go out and interview people on the street to get their opinions on a foreign policy shift by the new administration. Is it a smart move or a waste of time? What will the so-called "man on the street" or "vox pop" provide? Not much, you fear. You might counter that a certain executive with a local company used to be an ambassador to the region under a previous administration. This person might be an expert in that area and could be a valuable source.

When choosing the most powerful interviewee, you can probe four categories:

1. *Eyewitnesses.* Make every effort to find the authentic eyewitness and simply ask them to tell you what happened. Don't ask someone who only heard what happened or someone who was told something by an eyewitness, but find an actual observer of the event or tragedy. What is the better soundbite, a police officer telling us what someone else saw or the actual eyewitness?

2. *Experts on the topic.* You must be very careful that the expert you have chosen really knows the area of today's story. In jury trials it might

take an hour or so of questioning to qualify someone as an expert witness. Even if the person holds a title such as professor of chemistry, they may not be familiar with the particular story you are working on. Too often, experts who know little provide soundbites for stories because they are the only ones available and the deadline is near.

3. *Persons affected.* These include the person directly attacked or identified in the story. They are easy to identify.

4. *Someone who is part of a trend.* This is a common object for broadcast interviews. There's going to be a tax cut. Should you do a vox pop? Sure, because almost any person who pays taxes will be affected by the action. How about a recall of a brand of tires? Do you ask just any driver at the gas station for a response, or should you seek a car with that particular brand of tires?

Once you have the interviewee on the phone or are holding a mic in front of them, what do you ask? Remember, the research interview gets the data. So now its time for the soundbite interview. Your goal is to get the interviewee to respond in a manner that will give you effective soundbites in the area of the interviewee's qualifications. You should know what question you want the interviewee to answer before you even open your mouth. To get that answer, you should follow simple rules:

1. Listen to the answers. Repeat the questions if the interviewee is rambling, giving you incomplete answers, talking in jargon, or simply reciting statistics.

2. Be prepared to ask a tough question. To get a response to charges, you might have to say: "Some people have said you aren't up to the job of being city manager. How do you respond to those charges?"

3. Don't ask *yes* or *no* questions. Ask *how* or *why*. If you ask "Have you been effective as mayor?", she simply answers "Yes." Because we won't be using the reporter's questions, you have no effective soundbite. Instead, you might say "Can you tell us why you've been effective as mayor?"

    Now, suppose the "yes or no" question does slip out and the interviewee answers only "Yes." You should be prepared to immediately say "Why?"

Hunting for Sources

For each situation, name three persons from whom you could get a good recorded interview, and for each person write two questions that would stimulate a good broadcast bite. Write your questions on a separate page.

Situation 1

Your local planning commission is extending commercial zoning three blocks from the present limits into some residential neighborhoods.

Situation 2

Contaminated underground water is discovered in a local neighborhood. The samples contain chemicals used at a nearby metal-plating plant.

Situation 3

The late-night rock concert ended in a brawl, injuring two police officers and three concert goers. Now there's talk of ending the Pioneer Days event.

Situation 4

A health educator notes that new studies show too much coffee causes the brain to lose short-term memory.

Situation 5

School administrators hold an emergency neighborhood meeting for all parents whose children attend Park School. The police chief is there too. The officials will only say there is a dangerous situation.

PULLING BITES

Although a recorded broadcast interview is a lot of work, you cannot relax when it's over. Then it's time to start culling the stronger bites from the interview.

Now is the time when short interviews are virtues. If the Q-&-A goes on for 30 or 40 minutes, then you'll have to listen to all of the recording to find what you need. A 10-minute interview makes it easier to search, and in most cases, easier to remember if a usable bite is buried in there.

How Short a Bite?

The optimum length for a bite is always under discussion in broadcast. Some radio stations won't use anything more than :10; the same goes for certain television operations. Others say anything up to :20 is permissible. Still others leave it open-ended, relying on the content.

Often it depends upon the rise and fall of the vocal pitch, so the answer doesn't sound cut off, and whether or not the interviewee completes a sentence. It also reflects the talking and thinking speed of your source and it helps if he or she is not a member of the "Slow Talkers of America."

Many times this bite selection is done under intense deadline pressure. The reporter doesn't have time to listen to the entire interview but must go to a point where he or she thought there was a good answer. The bite must be isolated, and the story quickly written, so it all goes on the air within minutes. For this reason, it helps to make notes on the location of good answers in the interview. Some TV reporters carry microcassette recorders with them and listen to the playback while returning to the station.

When deadlines aren't forcing the issue, and you have days to edit the story, it helps to make a transcript of the entire interview. You may find that the interviewee never really answered the questions. You also may find second and third answers that are revealing on other topics and themes. You may find a powerful answer that is not expected, that changes the angle of the story. Transcripts are, however, a luxury and seldom available.

CUTTING BITES DOWN

Because you can paraphrase portions of an answer and put that into the writeup, you can trim the bites down to usable size. The best place to start is to eliminate the parenthetical pauses, "uhmms," and false starts at the beginning of the sentence. In this example, the underlined portions are the ones you are pulling.

Q: Why are the critics after you?
A: <u>Well...Uhmm...That's a good question.</u>
I think they...they are looking for a scapegoat because their convoluted and ill-conceived programs have all failed. And I'm it. Simple as the nose on your face...I called their bluff. <u>They needed...It's just like they didn't understand what I was doing.</u>

But if it still needs to be tighter, then trim from both the top and bottom. This requires more skill in the writeup, the sentence that prepares the audience for the upcoming soundbite.

> A: <u>I think they</u>...they are looking for a scapegoat because their convoluted and ill-conceived programs have all failed. And I'm it. <u>Simple as the nose on your face...I called their bluff.</u>

ETHICS

The first rule is to be very careful about the context of bites. In print, most interview bites are rebuilt from memory or scribble notes. In broadcast, it seems this wouldn't be a problem, because the answers are on audio or videotape. The problem, however, is context. By trimming the bite to its shortest form, reporters often eliminate qualifying statements and preconditions. If these aren't added in narration, then the story misrepresents the intent of the interviewee. Here's an example. Take this section from an interview:

> Q: What is your thinking about the latest incident?
> A: I've fought against violence for 20 years but I can still recognize that someone will honestly say 'I think that violence in this case was necessary.'

You simply cannot eliminate the first part of the answer and shorten the bite to the minimum. When this cut is made, a completely different answer would result.

> A: I think that violence in this case was necessary.

Second, answers should not be moved to another question. Maneuvering the questions and answers like freight cars may take them out of context. Although there is nothing wrong with using answers out of the original order, a problem occurs when the wrong question is linked to the wrong answer.

Third, avoid recording a better question after the interview. In radio this involves cutting in post-interview questions, and in television it means shooting reverse questions, done after the interview has ended and with the camera trained on the reporter. This technique is designed to help the reporter who stumbles through the question; however, it is hard to be accurate and usually results in a slightly different and more dramatic question. A better solution to a bad question is to paraphrase it in the writeup.

((• EXERCISE 5-B •))

Doing the Five-Minute Interview

Part 1

This assignment involves field work. Choose a story topic and angle for a local controversy. Research the topic and sum up the problem in one paragraph.

Select a person to interview about the topic. Contact that person, do a preinterview, and get permission for a recorded interview. You will use a small, cassette recorder and microphone.

Write out the objectives for answers from the recorded interview. Write out the questions you hope will stimulate those answers. Make a photocopy of the paragraph, the objectives, and the questions and turn those in as Part 1 of the assignment.

Part 2

After Part 1 of this assignment is in the instructor's hands, conduct a 5-minute interview, sticking to that time limit. See if you can stimulate the answers you want. If the interviewee doesn't answer your questions, try repeating the questions.

Transcribe the interview. Mark the bites you'd pull to make a story out of the interview answers. Explain why these bites have some power.

Hand in the transcription.

EXERCISE 5-C

Selecting Effective Bites

Review the following transcript. Identify one weak bite and two strong bites, mark them, and read for time. Be prepared to defend your selections. This situation involves the extension of commercial zoning into what used to be residential neighborhoods.

Q: How long have you lived in the neighborhood?

A: 30 years.

Q: Are you upset with the council's move?

A: Yes.

Q: Why?

A: You see...uh...my family has grown up and...uh. Well, the kids are gone now but my wife and I have lived in this neighborhood for almost 30 years. And it's been a nice place. And I don't see why they think that we should have commercial zoning, parking meters, and then, you know what's next, they'll be tearing down houses to put up stores. Look at these houses. People have put a lot of loving care into them. Families have grown up here. I don't know why we need more businesses in downtown Steeltown.

Q: I hear they're offering a lot of money for the homes?

A: My neighbors have been offered 20-thousand over the market price and I've even heard rumors that some have been offered 45-thousand over the current price. These homes are in the 250-thousand dollar range right now.

Q: Won't that help?

A: Well...that's what the business people of the city council think. Personally,they can take all that money and throw it in the river. This is my home. You notice they didn't vote to put businesses in their neighborhoods. It's just another case of the little guy getting shafted by the rich.

Q: You sound like you're ready to fight this?

A: We're getting a lawyer. We've already identified a few laws the council broke in this rezoning. We'll file appeals next Tuesday. We'll stall this in the courts. We'll take it to the Supreme Court if necessary.

Q: Thank you.

Selecting Effective Bites

Review this transcript. Identify one weak bite and two strong bites, mark them, and read for time. Be prepared to defend your selections. This interview is with a politician, Congresswoman Linda Belleweather, who was in a close election race.

Q: Thank you for doing this interview.

A: You're more than welcome.

Q: Why is the race so tight?

A: I'm not sure but we think it has a lot to do with my votes on gun control and money for schools. The pro-gun forces are campaigning very hard against me and misrepresenting my stand on gun control.

Q: How do they do that?

A: They say I favored taking guns away from citizens, and my vote wasn't anything about that.

Q: Still, you voted in favor of tighter gun registration laws at gun shows.

A: Yes, I did, and I would do it again. My friends who are peace officers asked me to stop hasty sales at the show. It seems they constantly deal with weapons traded at these shows. I believe in supporting the good judgement of the cops and sheriffs deputies in my district, no matter what other organizations have to say.

Q: Your opponent has also questioned your attendance at congressional sessions.

A: My opponent doesn't know what he's talking about. When you are at work in Washington D.C., you have many committee meetings, or meetings with constituents every day. Often that means you won't attend every general session of Congress, but then no one does. If my opponent gets to Washington, he certainly has a lot to learn.

CHAPTER SUMMARY

Placing a recorded statement in a news story has a severe impact on read-only stories. Reporters doing recorded interviews should concentrate on getting bites that are stronger than a written account could provide. These bites usually come in situations involving eyewitness accounts, professional evaluation, response to charges, and description of effects.

To select a bite, choose one that is short, concise, and with proper inflections in the voice. Ethical considerations forbid moving answers to another question or taking the bites out of context.

6

Using Soundbites Effectively

CHAPTER PREVIEW

The previous chapter was devoted to obtaining the most powerful and effective soundbite. This chapter focuses on using that soundbite in the most effective manner.

Most bites pulled from interviews will influence the construction of the story, from the lead sentence to the tag. In this book, the sentence immediately before the bite will be called the *writeup*. This writeup sentence makes the transition from a read-only story to an actuality, and provides the listener or viewer with an agenda for the bite. There are definite rules about the design of the writeup.

GLOSSARY

BACK-TO-BACK When soundbites from separate sources are edited together and are used without any narration.

COLD WRITEUP When a soundbite is inserted into a story without any introduction or identification of the speaker.

TAG A portion of copy, usually short, that follows an actuality or soundbite and ends the story. Also called an *out* or *outro*.

ADDING BITES CHANGES EVERYTHING

The decision to cut a recorded interview into smaller portions—called bites—and put one or more of those into a news story forces a radical change in the story structure. Because of the immediate needs of the bite in terms of how it fits into the narration, and because the bite's text influences the entire story, including the lead, the story must be planned with the interview bite in mind. Here's a situation that happens often in broadcast.

You've already finished a :25 reader on the new koalas at the zoo when the producer suggests that you use a :15 bite from a late interview with the zookeeper. The producer now is willing to give you :40 for the story. Is this a simple job, to insert the bite?

Not quite. The text of the bite is: "If that air conditioner isn't fixed, no one will be seeing any koalas. We'll have to send them right back where they came from."

Here's your original story. Find a spot to insert the bite.

> A BIG CIVIC TURNOUT TODAY TO WELCOME TWO SMALL VISITORS TO STEELTOWN.
>
> THE MAYOR...FOUR CITY COUNCIL MEMBERS AND THE BEAGLE HIGH BAND WERE AT THE FENTON ZOO AT NOON TO GREET A PAIR OF AUSTRALIAN KOALA BEARS.
>
> THE RARE ANIMALS ARE ON LOAN FROM THE ZOO IN SYDNEY. THEY'LL BE HERE FOR TWO MONTHS BUT IT'LL BE TWO WEEKS BEFORE THE PUBLIC CAN SEE THEM.
>
> IT TAKES THAT LONG FOR THE MALE AND FEMALE KOALA TO GET USED TO THEIR NEW CAGES.

Now, consider the bite you were given. It takes a different angle and shifts the focus from the cheerful welcome to malfunctioning equipment in the koala enclosure. The arrival of the koalas, treated lightly in the first copy story, now becomes a secondary angle in this story with a bite. The lead must refer to the possible problem with the koalas' new cage equipment.

To remedy the situation, you need more than a simple copyedit. You need:

1. a new lead

2. a new body for the story

3. a writeup for the quote

4. a place for the quote

5. a better description of the controversy

6. a suggestion of what might happen in the future

The new lead might sound like this:

> TWO LONG-AWAITED AUSTRALIAN VISITORS ARRIVED TODAY ONLY TO FIND THEIR ROOMS WEREN'T READY.
>
> THE RARE KOALA BEARS ARE IN STEELTOWN FOR A TWO-MONTH EXHIBIT AT THE FENTON ZOO.
>
> BUT THERE ARE PROBLEMS WITH THE SPECIAL ENCLOSURE PREPARED FOR THE POPULAR ANIMALS.
>
> ZOOKEEPER BRIAN ROSS SAYS EQUIPMENT BREAKDOWNS THREATEN THE EXHIBIT.
>
> "If that air conditioner isn't fixed, no one will be seeing any koalas. We'll have to send them right back where they came from."

ZOO OFFICIALS ARE HOPING FOR A QUICK SOLUTION. THE KOALAS ARE SCHEDULED FOR A REST PERIOD BEFORE THE EXHIBIT OPENS IN TWO WEEKS.

As you can see, the bite must be considered when writing the story. In a sense, soundbites and time restrictions force the design of the story, sometimes even changing the lead, but always by adding elements that take up time and need time-consuming introductory writeups and transitions back to the story narration or bridge between them.

PUTTING BITES INTO A STORY

Inserting a single bite into a story or inserting two bites back-to-back (edited together), forces a change in the story's design. In most cases, the bite or bites will cause everything, including the lead, to be rewritten. Bites will always need a smooth transition from the narrative, the writeup—the sentence immediately ahead of the bite.

Writeups

The writeup introduces the bite. Other news organizations have different names for this same device, whether it's the *intro, lead-in, wraparound,* or whatever. Use what local custom suggests. The rules for good writeups, however, stay the same, no matter what the terminology.

Rule 1. Keep the Interviewee's ID Close to the Bite. In any situation, the name and title of the interviewee should come within :05 of the bite—never any farther away than that. There are some newsrooms that like to put the ID immediately before the bite. Here are two examples; the first is generally used in television.

ZOOKEEPER LEONA WONG SAYS THAT IS NOT THE WAY KOALAS EAT. "We have spent a lot of money to ship in tons of..."

The second one is a traditional radio writeup. In radio, because there is no on-screen identifying title, the identification should go as close to the bite as possible.

AND THAT IS NOT THE WAY KOALAS EAT...SAYS ZOOKEEPER LEONA WONG.
"We have spent a lot of money to ship in tons of..."

While the ID for single bites is easy, multiple bites edited together present an ID problem. In radio this is much more difficult and often precludes using the bites together, unless the voices have already been introduced, become commonly known, or are easily identified by gender. If both speakers are introduced, then be very straightforward in identifying who speaks first.

In some situations, no identification is used. This is known as a cold intro and it works only in situations where it is clear who is speaking. Generally no ID is added when interviews are done on the street, vox pops.

Rule 2. Use a Short, Complete General Statement. This is a chance to give perspective to the recorded bite and help your listeners and viewers understand why the bite is in the story. It is unwise, although it is often done, to leave a half-completed statement and allow the actuality to finish it. Your writeup should be concise and clean.

> BUT GORDON SAYS THE KOALAS WON'T BE CHEAP TO KEEP. EVERYTHING MUST BE IMPORTED.
> "We have spent of lot of money to ship in tons of..."

This statement is really a manner of giving perspective to the bite that's coming up. If well done, it will help the viewer or listener adjust to the different voices and faces.

Rule 3. Avoid Repetition Between the Writeup and the First Sentence of the Bite. It is very easy to repeat words from the bite when you compose the writeup, especially under intense deadline pressure, because quite often you are relying only on your memory of what was in the interview. Your writeup will be stronger if you are careful to avoid this repetition. When there is a repetition, it throws away a chance to make a strong perspective statement immediately before the bite.

In this example, notice the repetition of the verb form *brought in:*

> ...THE KOALAS WON'T BE CHEAP TO KEEP. EVERYTHING MUST BE BROUGHT IN...
> "We have to bring in everything...tons of eucalyptus..."

In the next example, notice how the writer has changed the writeup to avoid the repetition.

> ...THE KOALAS WON'T BE CHEAP TO KEEP. EVERYTHING MUST BE IMPORTED.
> "We have to bring in everything...tons of eucalyptus..."

Rule 4. Avoid Throwaway Statements. A throwaway statement is an unneeded sentence or phrase that says nothing about the bite that is coming. Often, it praises your news-gathering efforts, such as "As she explained to our cameras." Avoid these. The example of a throwaway writeup is underlined.

AND AS ZOOKEEPER LEONA WONG SAYS...THE KOALAS WON'T BE CHEAP TO KEEP.
SHE DESCRIBED THE SITUATION THIS WAY.
"We have spent a lot of money to ship in tons of..."

Notice when the throwaway is deleted, it makes a stronger writeup that doesn't waste time.

AND AS ZOOKEEPER LEONA WONG SAYS...THE KOALAS WON'T BE CHEAP TO KEEP.
"We have spent a lot of money to ship in tons of..."

Rewrite for Writeups

Examine the four separate writeups in this story, identify the problems, find ways to strengthen each, and select the one you think makes the best link between the the first two sentences (the story) and the bite.

THE STATE IS STEPPING UP THE PRESSURE AGAINST DISHONEST USED CAR DEALERS.

TODAY THE LAWMAKERS PASSED THE LEMON BILL...REQUIRING A WINDOW STICKER ON ALL CARS.

(1) STATE CONSUMER AFFAIRS CHIEF SHARILEE WOOL SAYS SHE WILL NO LONGER FEEL SORRY FOR USED CAR BUYERS.

(2) STATE CONSUMER AFFAIRS CHIEF SHARILEE WOOL SAYS SOME WON'T GO TO THE TROUBLE OF READING THE WINDOW STICKER.

(3) STATE CONSUMER AFFAIRS CHIEF SHARILEE WOOL EXPLAINED IT THIS WAY TO US IN AN INTERVIEW WITH K-560 NEWS.

(4) STATE CONSUMER AFFAIRS CHIEF SHARILEE WOOL SAYS THIS LONG-AWAITED LEGISLATION ONLY GOES SO FAR.

> Bite: "Although this has been a long time coming and is a godsend, some still won't read the window sticker."

GETTING OUT OF THE BITE: THE TAG

A section of the story called the *tag* returns from the last soundbite back to the newscaster. This is a good place for a number of items. First, put information in the tag that didn't fit into the story before the bite. Second, the interviewee can be re-identified, something more useful in radio. Start the tag with his or her name: "CLARK ALSO SAID..."

Last, you can smooth the continuity by using repetition. Choose a key-word or phrase from the last sentence of the bite and repeat it in the first sentence of the news copy after the bite. In this example, the phrase is "solving the parking mess."

> "...and I just don't see how this will help <u>solve the parking mess</u>."
> BUT <u>SOLVING THE PARKING MESS</u> WASN'T THE ONLY PRIORITY FOR
> THE CITY'S TEAM.
> THEY HAD TO...

PLACEMENT OF THE BITES WITHIN STORIES

Ideally, the bite should be placed in the story to allow a studio portion before the bite and a studio tag after the bite. In most cases, the portion before the bite is longer than the tag.

Opening with the bite is extremely difficult. An actuality dislocates the audience from the familiar voice of the newscaster. If the bite is too close to the top, it is hard to include sufficient perspective or compose enough attribution for the audience to make sense out of the change in voice or picture.

By the same token, ending on a bite can cause problems. Without at least a one sentence tag after the bite, you leave open the chance that the audience will not be able to separate this bite from the beginning of the next story.

(((EXERCISE 6-B)))

Using Bites

Go back to the interviews in Exercises 5-C and 5-D of the last chapter (with the gentleman facing rezoning of his neighborhood and with Congresswoman Belleweather). Select a concise bite from each one. Position each in the middle of a blank piece of paper and write a story (about :30 total) around the bite. Be sure that the writeups conform to the rules.

Using the Five-Minute Interview

Return to Exercise 5-B from the last chapter in which you recorded a five-minute interview and prepared a transcript. From the transcript, pick three good sound-bites, and write three :20 stories, placing one of those soundbites in each story. Use a separate sheet of paper.

CHAPTER SUMMARY

Using soundbites changes the design and structure of a news story. Writers who know they have a soundbite should design the story around its content. Writers should be careful to follow the four simple rules of effective writeups leading into the bite: (a) keep the ID close to the bite; (b) use a short, complete general statement; (c) avoid repetition; and (d) avoid throwaway statements. Writers should make the most out of the tag, leading out of the soundbite. It is a good device for re-identification, for repetition, and for adding bits of information to the story. Finally, try not to either open or close your story with a bite.

7

Using Soundbites in Packages

CHAPTER PREVIEW

This chapter covers the construction of stories (using soundbites) that are written to be read by a reporter and not a studio anchor. One focus is the lead-in, which must attract the attention of the viewer and funnel attention to the specifics of the story. The chapter also explores various narrative models, including the altered chronology, the particular-to-general, and the payoff.

GLOSSARY

ALTERED CHRONOLOGY A narrative model that flows from the studio lead-in to the present time frame, then to the past, then to the controversy or points of story development, and then ends with the future.

LEAD-IN Studio newscaster's introduction to a field report narrated by another reporter. Lead-ins are short, :10 or so, and should be written by the reporter to coordinate the introduction.

PARTICULAR-TO-GENERAL A narrative model that flows from the studio lead-in to a particular case, then to the general trend, then to the evaluation or future, and may end up by returning to wrap up the elements of the initial particular case. It is also called *personalization.*

REMOTE A story done by the reporter live while at a location other than the newsroom studio.

TRACK A portion of a reporter's narration for a report from the field. Tracks are usually scripted and recorded in the newsroom. A field package might contain many tracks, with each track separating other elements, such as SOTs. Thus the narration between the story's beginning and the first bite is track 1, between the first bite and the second bite is track 2, between the second bite and the end of the story is track 3, and so on.

VOICER A radio report, narrated by someone other than the newscaster, that does not contain a bite or other actuality. A voicer is usually recorded and played back from a cart.

WRAP Also called the *wraparound, wrapper, takeout, insert,* or *package.* This is a radio reporter's story from the field that includes bites of actuality within it.

LONGER FORMAT NARRATIVE WRITING

In Chapter 6, we explored the read-only story and the studio-based story wrapped around a single actuality or soundbite. Now we shift to stories reported by someone other than the anchor/newscaster. These stories often combine a studio segment lead-in with a package of ambient sound, reporter tracks, and interview bites. When assembling the longer stories, the reporter picks and chooses from among those pieces and hooks one to another until the story is told within the time allotted. A crucial point in the story construction is the writeup; writers should follow the rules for that from Chapter 6.

THE FUNCTION OF A LEAD-IN

Almost every radio and television field report is preceded by a studio introduction, read by the newscaster, called a *lead-in.* If the lead-in is carefully written, it can both provide information and carry the audience to the opening of the field report.

A lead-in has many functions. First, the lead-in's function is to prepare the ground, not tell the story. If it gives a short version of the story, why should the listeners or viewers wait for the field report?

Second, it serves as an attention-narrowing funnel, with the wide view in the first sentence and a more specific focus immediately before the reporter's voicer, wrap, remote, or package. The first sentence is general perspective on the story.

Third, the lead-in is a place to put story information crucial to the story that might not fit in the field report. This often is an update of the story, which works well as the lead-in to a backgrounder. In a television report, the lead-in is also the place to put nonvisual information that did not fit comfortably in the report.

Last, the lead-in identifies the next voice: either that of the reporter, or if the field report opens with a bite before the first track, then that of the speaker. The amount of identification used often varies with station news policy.

Here's a sample lead-in. Notice the first sentence offers perspective. It casts a wide net for viewers who might be generally interested in the story. The second sentence, which includes the reporter's identifier, bridges from that overview to the details in track 1.

FOR CENTURIES ZOOS HAVE GIVEN OUR CITY DWELLERS A QUICK LESSON IN EXOTIC WILD ANIMALS...

BUT TODAY'S NEW ARRIVALS AT FENTON ZOO ARE HARDLY EXOTIC...AND AS MIRIAM MCKENNA REPORTS...THEY MIGHT BE CALLED CUDDLY.

(Track #1) "Zoo visitors got their first look today at the brother-sister duo of giant pandas...on loan from the Washington Zoo."

Not all stories need to start with perspective and then narrow to the particular elements that lead to the story. For backgrounders, the lead-in would use a breaking news story with a similar theme and then segue to the field package with the reporter's ID. That's a common practice when stations have stories on the shelf, known as *HFR* (hold for release) or *banked stories*.

For features, the lead-in can be long, sweeping, and highly stylized and use clever wordplay. It is less direct and tends more toward narrative storytelling.

TRACKS

The First Track

Anyone writing wrap or package scripts should be aware of the importance of providing the correct amount of story background. If it wasn't in the lead-in, then it should be in the first track. Often, the first track is a bit longer than the others, but if details are needed to give the scope of the story, this is where they should go. It should be written after the lead-in.

The soundbites you have chosen should now be arranged in the order you want.

The Middle Tracks

Middle tracks are often useful as bridges from one soundbite to the next. It is always good to segue into the track with some slight repetition from the end of the previous bite.

Middle tracks set the pace for the package. The shorter they are, the faster the story moves. Some reporters like to keep these interior tracks very short.

Cold writeups (or no writeups) can be used in the middle tracks, especially if the speaker has appeared in an earlier bite.

The Last Track

The last track is traditionally the place for leftover information and for the future path of the story. When spelling out the next step for the story, try to avoid clichés such as "Only time will tell" and "Who knows what will happen next?" See if you, the reporter, can find out hard information about the next step.

ALTERED CHRONOLOGY MODEL

The altered chronology model is usually used with a hard news or breaking story. In this case, it is useful to take story elements out of their natural chronology. The altered time sequence of lead-in, present, past, controversy, and future provides a good model. Bites are kept short.

1. *Lead-in.* Begins with perspective but shifts to set up the time of the report.

THERE'S BEEN A TURNAROUND IN THE FORTUNES OF A LOCAL CHARITY.
REPORTER BOB WATSON SAYS THE NEW MOOD AT STEELTOWN FUND IS UPBEAT.

2. *Wrap script.*

(Track #1—present) THERE WERE BIG SMILES TODAY AT THE STEELTOWN FUND OFFICES.
(Track #1—background) THE 1994 CORPORATE FUND DRIVE PICKED UP 31-MILLION DOLLARS IN PLEDGES...ALMOST DOUBLE LAST YEAR'S TOTAL.
THE STAFF REACHED THAT GOAL DESPITE THE SUMMER'S PROBLEMS...WITH A SPECIAL AUDIT AND CHARGES OF MISMANAGEMENT.
EXECUTIVE DIRECTOR MARY WILLIAMS SAYS IT TOOK TIME TO OVERCOME THE PROBLEMS.
(Soundbite #1) "We were pretty low six months ago, but we stayed focused on this year's goal and that helped. Now we've really had a successful year."
(Track #2—controversy) BUT SUCCESS THIS YEAR WON'T MAKE THE CONTROVERSY GO AWAY. THERE STILL MAY BE OVER A MILLION DOLLARS MISSING...AND SHERIFF'S DETECTIVE MIKE STONE IS STILL INVESTIGATING.
(Soundbite #2) "We've been working on this for six months and we should wrap it up next week."
(Track #3) SO WHILE THE STAFF AT THE STEELTOWN FUND WAIT FOR THE OTHER SHOE TO DROP...THEY CAN START HANDING OUT THE 31-MILLION IN AID. THAT SHOULD BEGIN IN THE NEXT TWO MONTHS.
FOR K-560 NEWS...THIS IS BOB WATSON AT THE STEELTOWN FUND OFFICES.

Using the Altered Chronology Model

Write a :10 newscaster lead-in and a three-track reporter's narration for this situation. Structure the report around the altered chronology model.

Situation

The controversy goes back to a planning commission agreement to allow a fast food franchise to move into an old, ornate bank building. The hamburger chain was going to sell burgers and fries from the old tellers' windows. The fast food company spent nearly $900,000 converting the structure, but a local neighborhood conservation group smelled a deal cooking and filed suit to stop the franchise. They want a local judge to order an environmental impact report and stop the conversion. Today, your reporter is at the courthouse where Judge Dale Hart is hearing the case.

The attorneys for the conservation group presented a petition signed by 80 percent of the 1,400 families in the neighborhood, asking that the planning commission action be reconsidered. The judge has promised to rule by next week.

The spokesperson for the fast food chain told reporters that legally there is nothing the judge can do to stop the move, unless there was fraud by city officials.

Soundbite from hamburger company spokesperson Rhonda Biftek: "We followed all the rules and have all the permits. It's time to let us build."

Soundbite from the protestors (neighborhood activist Mona Nimby): "No one knew anything about it until last week's meeting. There's been a coverup."

PARTICULAR-TO-GENERAL MODEL

Personalizing stories provides another useful model, especially for backgrounders and features. It begins with a particular case, then moves to a general trend, and then returns to the particular case. To use this model, take a story of general trends or widespread effects (for example, layoffs at a local plant) and find someone who is personally affected. The lead-in is general but funnels the viewer interest directly to the individual's story. The reporter's first track starts with the focus on the individual. Then the story reverts back to the general trend, discusses any controversy and future, and may end with final details on the individual's case.

This type of model has drawbacks, notably when the focus gets too wide or when you choose a person to exemplify the story who is not representative of most of those affected by the situation.

Production of the story can also be overambitious. You can minimize this problem by reducing the number of interviewees, the number of bites per interviewee, and the number of topics in the focus.

Here's an example of this particular-to-general model, also known as personalization. The lead-in begins with perspective but moves quickly to the person featured in the report.

> THERE ARE RUMORS THE LOCAL THOMAS WINDOW FACTORY MAY CLOSE...AND AS BOB WATSON REPORTS...IF IT DOES...ONE WOMAN AND HER FAMILY WILL BE BIG LOSERS.

The track for the voicer begins with a concentration on the woman.

> LISA PETERSEN HAS WORKED AT THE THOMAS WINDOW ASSEMBLY PLANT IN STEELTOWN FOR THE PAST 14 YEARS.
> SHE'S NOW A LINE MANAGER...AND AS A SINGLE PARENT...LISA PETERSEN SAYS HER PAYCHECK IS VITAL FOR HER FAMILY.
> (Soundbite #1) "We're about one week away from being flat broke."
> BUT LISA HAS HEARD SHE'S ON THE LIST TO BE LAID-OFF...AND SO ARE 18-HUNDRED OF HER CO-WORKERS.
> IT'S A LOSS THAT WILL BE DEVASTATING FOR THE INDUSTRIAL SECTION OF STEELTOWN. TWO OTHER PLANTS CLOSED WITHIN THE PAST YEAR.
> MAYOR CARLY ROGERS SAYS THIS LATEST SHUTDOWN WILL BE A SEVERE BLOW
> (Soundbite #2) "This is going to devastate the city. We've been hit before, but this is a big one. The company had better help out."
> COMPANY OFFICIALS AREN'T SAYING WHO WILL BE LET GO... EXCEPT TO SAY THERE WILL BE AN ANNOUNCEMENT FRIDAY.
> LISA PETERSEN ISN'T WAITING. SHE'S TAKEN SOME DAYS OFF AND IS OUT LOOKING FOR WORK. BOB WATSON FOR K-560 NEWS.

Particular-to-General Script

Write a :10 newscaster lead-in and a three-track reporter's narration for this situation. Structure the report around the particular-to-general model discussed in this section.

Situation

The Consumer Product Safety Commission has ordered the recall of over 2 million home treadmill machines made by the El Molino Company of Mexico. The treadmills, which are used by fitness buffs, have a regulator that keeps the speed of the belt constant. But the federal officials say that on El Molino's Model X200, the regulators were faulty and the motor can speed up the treadmill to 25 miles-per-hour and prevent the exerciser from stopping it. Already, there have been over 100 reported injuries from the treadmills, many of them serious. El Molino says it will repair the faulty treadmills if people will bring them to its facility in Monterrey, Mexico.

Morris Souhem, a 37-year-old St. Louis attorney, bought one of the treadmills and used it for two months before the morning he went flying off it and was thrown into the wall, breaking his leg.

(Soundbite #1) "These are criminally dangerous, and the company didn't test the regulators but instead bought them sight unseen from the surplus military market."

(Soundbite #2—Marvin Feetness, a dealer in El Molino treadmills) "We are sorry that this happened and we are offering to replace anyone's faulty model."

PAYOFFS

Other prominent elements of narrative can be useful for features and back-grounders. A payoff model builds the sense of mystery and natural drama by releasing small bits of information about the story a little at a time, while alerting the audience that the important information is to come later.

Broadcast writers may use this technique for two reasons. First, it helps them hold the audience's attention. If the audience heard the whole story at once, they might tune out if they weren't really interested. Second, audiences find it easier to retain information if it is given in small amounts.

Payoff Story Model

This model skirts the edge of sensationalism, and payoff users must be careful. In this format, you boldly lead the audience on, more or less promising that the payoff is forthcoming.

(Lead-in)

IT WASN'T UNUSUAL THAT A POSTAL WORKER HAD A SIX-YEAR-OLD FOLLOW HIM AROUND WHILE HE DELIVERED THE MAIL.

BUT AS HAMID MASHAHAN REPORTS...THIS YOUNGSTER WAS SPECIAL.

(Track #1—present)

IN FACT...THE SIX-YEAR-OLD CRACKED A FEW SIDEWALKS IN THE FAIRVIEW SECTION OF TOWN WHILE TAGGING AFTER CARRIER BOB JENKINS ON HIS APPOINTED ROUNDS. THE LOCAL KIDS WERE HAPPY.

(Soundbite #1) "He sure is big."

AND WHILE BOB CAREFULLY PLACED THE LETTERS AND PACKAGES IN THE MAIL SLOTS...THE SIX-YEAR-OLD SCATTERED PEANUT SHELLS BEHIND...DELIGHTING EVEN MORE OF THE CHILDREN.

(Soundbite #2) "I wish I had some peanuts for him."

BOB'S FRIEND ON THE ROUTE TODAY WAS A CIRCUS ELEPHANT NAMED ROXIE...ALONG WITH HER HANDLER LOUISE ALLSMELL. IT'S ALL PART OF A PROMOTION FOR THE ROCKET CIRCUS DUE IN TOWN NEXT WEEK. THIS IS BOB WATSON FOR K-560 NEWS.

((• EXERCISE 7-C •))

Package With Payoff

Write a payoff model script with a lead-in and a three-track, two-soundbite structure reporting the situation below.

Situation

Lottery winner Alfred Komp finally showed up today with the winning ticket. He had just 24 hours left until the time ran out. The prize—$12.3 million, spread out in checks over 20 years. Komp was a week late in claiming the prize. He said he had to retrace his route to Lake Shasta, where he had vacationed for a week with his family. He had to stop at each of the six motels where the family had stayed on the vacation, and go through each of the drawers.

Finally, in the last one, at the Lost Horizons in Bellvue, he found the ticket behind the nightstand. Komp says he will quit work and live the leisure life now that he has the money.

Chapter Summary

Longer reports from the field, usually voiced by reporters, have many narrative elements that need a usable order. This chapter explores the basic models of altered chronology, the particular-to-general, and the payoff, all with soundbites.

8

Over-the-Air and Internet Radio

CHAPTER PREVIEW

News is a common staple of many radio stations and is certainly a vital element of a station's Internet offerings. The earlier chapters of this book cover writing styles that will work in both radio or television. This chapter's highlights take you through various over-the-air radio formats and also explore the surprising world of Internet radio.

A distinction can be drawn between a radio news story designed for the studio newscaster's voice (the anchor) and those stories reported by other staff members, generally from events taking place in the field. In the studio, stories are called *readers* or *actualities.* Field report formats include the *voicer,* which is the reporter's recorded narration without any actuality; the *wrap,* which is a composite of the reporter's recorded narration and bites from actualities; the *Q-&-A;* and the *remote,* which is done live by way of a car phone, cellular phone, or special hookup.

GLOSSARY

AUDIO BILLBOARD   A verbal identifier placed at the head of each take of each track that is recorded. Also known as a *slate,* it includes the story slug, the track number, the take number, and a countdown. An example would be "Bus crash...Track One...Take One...Coming in three...two...one..."

CART   A plastic case with enclosed tape that is used to play back actualities, voicers, and other recordings for radio newscasts. Carts come in many lengths and are easy to load and easy to cue. Sometimes, the term *cart* is loosely applied to any recorded element to be used in a newscast.

HFR   (stands for *hold for release*) A story that is finished but is being saved for a later program or date. Also called an *evergreen* or a *banked* story.

Q-&-A   Live question and answer session between studio anchor and reporter in the field. Also known as a debrief.

REMOTE A story done by the reporter live while the reporter is at another location.

ROUND ROBIN A series of reports, usually done live, in which the studio anchor starts by tossing to one field reporter who tosses to the next, who tosses to the next, and so on.

SERVER A local network computer hub that stores scripts, copy, and in more complex systems, the actualities.

SLATE Same as billboard

VOICER A report, narrated by someone other than the newscaster, that does not contain a bite or other actuality. A voicer is usually recorded and played back from a cart.

WRAP Also called the *wraparound, wrapper, takeout, insert,* or *package.* This is a reporter's recorded story from the field that includes bites of actuality within it.

THE CHANGING WORLD OF RADIO

The radio news world is broken into distinct operations, each of which determines how you will format and write your stories. For over-the-air radio, there are network feeds and syndications, local major-market all-news operations, small commercial music/news format stations, and noncommercial public or listener-supported stations.

In the Internet realm, there are thousands of over-the-air stations that re-feed their signal over the Internet; there are stations devoted solely to Internet broadcasting similar to over-the-air; there are so-called content providers or syndicators who specialize in niche broadcasting on the Internet and who also sell features to the thousands of radio stations nationwide.

All of these formats offer the radio news writer/reporter/anchor a different challenge, from news reports that are designed for the tightly formatted news wheels of major-market commercial all-news to those of the loosely formatted wraps of the noncommercial station.

RADIO'S SMALL STAFFS

Although radio news is the first source of immediate information for most Americans, it is usually prepared and presented by a skeleton staff of journalists. A year 2000 Radio Television News Director's Association survey estimated there were only 11,600 full-time and 800 part-time radio journalists in the country—for more than 10,000 stations. While a large all-news major-market station may have 30 in the newsroom, the average music/news format station has a news staff of one to four, in which reporter/anchors write each broadcast, call for recorded interviews, bring in and break down actuality feeds, and act as newscasters. This leaves little time for field reporting, although some mixed-format station journalists work half-days in the field. Many free-lancers work alone and sell stories or features to syndicators, who pass them along to stations or Internet broadcasters.

REPORTS FROM THE FIELD

Radio field reporting is done either under intense and immediate deadline pressure or, in the case of profiles, reviews, and HFR backgrounders, within a much more relaxed schedule.

Unlike the television reporter, the radio reporter usually works alone. This can make the job more difficult because the reporter must wear two hats: the information processing reporter and the technician who handles the details like the mic placement and recording levels. But as any radio reporter knows, the decisive personal control over most of the reporting process and the story in radio provides a sense of accomplishment.

As a radio reporter, you'll face problems. There are constant deadlines that require filing over the cell phone, regular wired phone, proprietary two-way radio, or even the Internet. You'll have to write scripts in the field, sometimes in noisy and distracting environments. You'll also be overburdened with stories and hard pressed to do as complete a job as you would like. Still, the field work is a satisfying part of journalism.

In the studios, you'll have scripts for readers and actualities (or *R/A* as they are noted in some stations). The most-used field report formats are the voicer, the wrap, Q-&-As, and the remote.

KEY ELEMENTS OF WRITING FOR RADIO

Over-the-air radio has been called the theater of the mind, because good writers can conjure up images for listeners. But most radio news is heavily formatted into tiny story slots, so the possibility of eloquent writing sometimes evaporates into :10 stories and :25 wraps. Consequently, rules particular to radio are

1. *You must be descriptive.* Obviously, the visuals aren't there, so you have to add words that speak of sights, sounds, aromas, and whatever else contributes to setting the scene. Ambient sound is often a big help to accomplishing word pictures.

2. *You must write tightly.* Scripts are short. Commercial radio network newscasts are brutal, with stories ranging from :10 to :30. This demands that you winnow out the excess material and include only what is necessary to tell the story. Noncommercial newscasts are longer, but often are formatted into tight patterns.

3. *You can write with more style.* Your vocal presentation must be gracious and authoritative, and your personal warmth must come through in your reports.

RADIO NEWS SCRIPTS

Because radio does not employ a large control room staff, the scripts do not need extensive technical information. Printers now commonly produce the script pages, which generally extend across the page with 1-inch margins. This gives a four-second line, so a :30 story would be about eight lines. Double space between the lines makes it easier to read, although some newsrooms require triple-spaced intervals.

Technical information is usually a matter of indicating which cart or hard disk source you'll be using, whether or not it is cued, what the incue and the outcue are, and what the TRT is on the actuality. The following is an example of a radio script.

TRAIN/jnh/6pm

NATIONAL TRANSPORTATION SAFETY BOARD INVESTIGATORS SAY A BROKEN RAIL MAY HAVE CAUSED THE DEADLY AMTRAK ACCIDENT NEAR OXFORD MISSISSIPPI.

THE NEW REPORT SAYS A MAINTENANCE CREW ATTEMPTED TO FIX THE TROUBLE SPOT EARLIER THAT DAY.

SAFETY SPECIALIST AMIN RAHSHUK SAYS THE TRAIN CREW NEVER HAD A CHANCE.

(Cart #22B TRT :26)

IC: "The engine was going 60 miles-an-hour..."

EC: "...Never knew what hit him."

THE ACCIDENT LAST WEEK LEFT TWO DEAD AND THREE SERIOUSLY INJURED.

Notice that each cart or disk source includes a tape running time, or TRT, an incue and an outcue, and depending upon the particular station, might also include a précis of the soundbite or a verbatim transcript. The précis or text of the bite are invaluable to the newscaster when the dreaded moment arrives when the wrong cart or disk comes up.

In radio, with a script readied by the newscaster, any technical information is generally circled to indicate that it shouldn't be read.

THE VOICER

A voicer is a field reporter's narration of a story without an actuality. Although this term usually refers to a report on a cart, it can be applied to a live story. Voicers are usually short, from :30 to 1:00. They are preceded by a studio lead-in, which may be anywhere from :05 to :10, depending on the station's style.

Here's an example of a voicer script. The anchor lead is a segue after other fire stories.

Lead-in:

WITH ALL THOSE FIRES BURNING THIS YEAR...OFFICIALS GAVE OUR REPORTER KIM CLARK A LESSON ON FIRE SAFETY.

Voicer script on cart:

(ON CART)...(NAT SOT...WHOOSH OF FLAMES)
THAT'S THE SOUND OF FLAMES ROARING THROUGH DRY BRUSH... ALL PART OF A BLAZING DEMONSTRATION TODAY BY THE SAN CLEMENTE HILLS FIRE DEPARTMENT.
THEY BURNED AN OLD PATCH OF WEEDS BEHIND THE FIREHOUSE TO DEMONSTRATE JUST HOW EXPLOSIVE WILDFIRES CAN BE THIS YEAR.
FIRE CAPTAIN LARRY ANDERSON SAYS EARLY AND HEAVY RAINS ARE RESPONSIBLE. THERE'S MORE LOW UNDERBRUSH THAN IN A NORMAL YEAR AND THAT MEANS THERE'S MORE FUEL WAITING FOR A SPARK.
ANDERSON WANTS HILLSIDE HOMEOWNERS TO MAKE AN EFFORT THIS YEAR TO CUT BACK BRUSH WITHIN 50 FEET OF THEIR HOMES. HE ALSO WARNED AGAINST PILING THAT REFUSE NEAR THE HOUSES. OTHERWISE...HE SAYS HIS CREWS ARE IN FOR A BUSY SUMMER. THIS IS KIM CLARK FOR K-560 NEWS.

Notice the altered chronology development of the story. The reporter explains the current situation (at the fire demonstration), then the background (heavy rains, lots of brush), then the controversy/story advance (cut the brush), and then the future (busy summer).

Writing Lead-ins and Voicers

Write a :10 lead-in and a :45 voicer for this situation. Remember what purpose the lead-in serves.

Situation

It is election day and you have a voicer due on a newscast at 11 a.m. It is now 10:30 and your report is supposed to tell the story of the early hours of election day.

All morning long, you were at Precinct 19, which is in Lowbrau Elementary School. At that precinct, there was a mix-up about who was supposed to bring the keys to open up the polling place, so instead of opening at 8 a.m., it opened at 9:15, and people who wanted to vote before work were angry.

Usually, Precinct 19 has 250 voters by 10 a.m., but this morning, because of the problem, there were only 13. There are 620 registered voters in Precinct 19.

In the rest of the city, the vote totals are low, according to the registrar, and the overall voter turnout is only expected to total 45 percent for the election. The candidates are running for two city council seats and a school board spot.

THE REMOTE

With the technology now available to receive a clear line from almost anywhere, it's a sure bet that radio reporters will be doing more live remote broadcasts. This might be a simple voicer, a Q-&-A, or a complex two- to three-minute description of a scene including the replay of an actuality.

Doing a remote can be strenuous. After the clear line is set up, you must wait patiently for the newscasters to come to you, even if the nice quiet situation that you set up is deteriorating into a noisy, crowded group of kibitzers. If you're on the phone, it's a sure bet that someone will want the line.

Here are some suggestions to help on your first few remotes.

1. Make certain you and the producer agree about what part of the story you will be doing. Find out what information will be given before and during the lead-in, and where you are expected to pick up the report. If this is a round robin, you must know where you pick up from one reporter and toss to another, and what areas they will cover.

2. Script your report as fully as you can. Sometimes you'll have to improvise, but if possible, know exactly what you'll be saying. There are too many distractions in the field to wing every remote.

3. If necessary, use a narrative model. The altered chronology (lead-in/present/past/controversy/future), the particular-to-general (lead-in/particular case/general trend/developments-future/particular case), and the cause-and-effect models can be useful.

4. If you will be playing back a bite from an interview, be certain that you've recued the tape. If you've already fed the bite and they are playing the cart from the studio, give them both the roll cue and how far into the piece the cart will play.

5. When you finish, stand by for a possible Q-&-A session with the newscaster, even if that hadn't been planned. Sudden needs at the studio or new twists of the story might require the answer to a question that's been left unanswered.

A typical remote might go like this.

Anchor:

WE HAVE WORD THE SUPERVISORS JUST VOTED TO END A LIFE-SAVING SERVICE.
REPORTER GUY HAMILTON IS STANDING BY WITH THE STORY. GUY?

Reporter:

ROGER...AT THE MOMENT THE SUPERVISORS ARE TAKING A BREAK. BUT BEFORE THEY LEFT...ABOUT 20-MINUTES AGO...THEY VOTED TO CUT THE FUNDS FOR THE COUNTY'S AMBULANCE SERVICE.
THAT ACTION MIGHT PROVE TO BE A BIT UNPOPULAR...AND THE CROWD HERE WAS AGAINST IT.

THE MOVE TO SHUT DOWN THE SERVICE BEGAN FOUR MONTHS AGO...AFTER SOME PRIVATE FIRMS SAID THEY COULD DO AS GOOD A JOB...BUT FOR LESS MONEY. WELL...A COMMITTEE CHECKED OUT THAT CLAIM AND AGREED...RECOMMENDING TO END THE COUNTY'S PARTICIPATION. SUPERVISOR GUSTAVO RODRIGUEZ SAYS IT'S A MATTER OF MONEY.

CART #1 TRT :20
IC: "We have to be..."
EC: "...for everyone."

THE CUTOFF BECOMES EFFECTIVE NEXT WEEK. AND THE PRIVATE AMBULANCE OPERATORS SAY THEY'LL BE READY. THIS IS GUY HAMILTON REPORTING LIVE FROM THE COUNTY BUILDING.

((• EXERCISE 8-B •))

Remote Practice

This exercise involves finding a story in the field, writing it there, and calling it in. This is what you do.

You will be assigned a meeting or event to cover, whether it is a city council, school board, planning commission, special day for special guests, or whatever. You must do some research, then attend that event to report on what occurred.

At the conclusion of the event, you must write up a remote voicer, :45-1:00, in which you follow the altered chronology model (present/past/controversy or development/future). You will also suggest a lead-in. If you can't think of one, remember that the first sentence or lead to your story can be turned into a lead-in.

The instructor will set up a time and phone number for you to call, and your story will be put on tape. Before you read it over the phone, you must put an audio billboard (verbal slugline) at the top of each take, plus a countdown. A billboard goes like this.

CITY COUNCIL...YOUR NAME...TAKE NUMBER (one, two...etc.) COMING IN...THREE...TWO...ONE...

Then, feed the voicer. If you make even one mistake, give another billboard and start immediately.

Your voicer should also have a tag or standard closing on it. It will probably include your name, your location, and your station.

THE Q-&-A

The Q-&-A is a report that allows the field reporters to add more information based on their knowledge of a particular situation. Within a time framework, you'll be able to expand on story points, give insider perspective, and generally provide the most convincing examples of reporting. There are a few pitfalls, though:

1. The anchor should be aware of what the reporter doesn't know about. That will prevent the embarrassing unanswered question.

2. The anchor and reporter should agree on the area for the first question. Sometimes it is scripted, but more often it is ad libbed from a suggested topic.

3. The anchor, who is sitting isolated in an announce booth at the station, should be aware of difficult conditions at the reporter's location. If there's a crowd there, sometimes an unruly one, then the anchor must be cautious about continuing the remote for too long a time.

THE WRAP

A wrap (or wraparound) is a field story format that differs from the voicer because it contains at least one and usually more actualities. Sometimes the term *wraparound* is used for any story in which a presenter's voice wraps around an actuality.

Although there are a bewildering variety of models for wraps, the general narrative models discussed in Chapter 7 can guide you in preparing these. Try either the altered chronology model or the particular-to-general model. The wrap involves a lot of planning for the flow of the narrative. It also involves planning a writeup for each bite and a number of tracks. It is involved and should be practiced as often as possible.

Strategies for Wraps

A wrap always begins with the lead-in, which is given by the newscaster in the studio. The transcript of the tracks used in the voicers and wraps are seldom included in the newscaster's scripts. Some stations require that a short synopsis or précis be added to the bottom of the lead-in script page. In many stations the scripts for the tracks are kept and filed; other stations keep airchecks (recordings) of the stories.

A script for a wrap is broken into many parts, and usually alternates track-bite-track, and so on. If you are a new reporter out on one of your first stories, it's a good idea (if there's time) to project ahead and attempt to write the story before you cover it. Although the story is bound to change when you get there, this exercise will give you advance warning what your needs might be. Start with the lead-in, trying to determine what will attract the audience to this story.

Remember, the best angle or peg will probably be the topic that interested you in the story. It must also have some perspective.

A caution here: Pre-writing is only an exercise. In the field, a story may be different, have a different angle, or be no story at all.

This script is an example of a short, two-bite wrap.

Lead-in:

MUSEUMS ALWAYS SEEM TO BE SHORT OF FUNDS BUT NOW A LOCAL CENTER HAS SOLVED THAT PROBLEM...AT LEAST FOR THIS YEAR. CARRIE LISH HAS THE STORY.

Track #1

ROBERT HALL IS THE SUPERVISING DIRECTOR FOR THE BENTON MODERN ART MUSEUM AND HE'S A HAPPY MAN THIS MORNING.

IN FACT...HE WAS BEAMING WHEN REPORTERS SHOWED UP IN HIS OFFICE FOR A MORNING NEWS CONFERENCE. HE SAYS AN ANONYMOUS DONOR GAVE 195-THOUSAND DOLLARS TO THE MUSEUM... ENOUGH TO RUN THE FACILITY FOR A YEAR. HALL SAYS THAT SOLVES A CRISIS.

Bite #1

"We were desperate. This couldn't have come at a better time. Our insurance has tripled in the past year and we might have closed. This will give us some breathing room."

Track #2

HALL SAYS THE DONOR WANTS TO REMAIN IN THE BACKGROUND BUT THAT SHE IS A LOCAL MERCHANT.

Bite #2

"She walked in the office one day and said she had heard stories about our problems. She just took out her checkbook and wrote out a check for the amount. We were certainly relieved that the crisis was over."

Track #3

BUT THE RELIEF WON'T LAST LONG. HALL SAYS THE MUSEUM STAFF HAS TO USE THIS WINDFALL AS A BREATHER SO THAT FUNDRAISING FOR NEXT YEAR CAN BEGIN.

AND THAT...HE SAYS...WILL BEGIN NEXT MONDAY.

AT THE MODERN ART MUSEUM...THIS IS CARRIE LISH FOR K-560 NEWS.

Writing the Wrap

Write a :10 lead-in and a 1:20 wrap for this situation.

SITUATION

You have three actualities on a story about global warming. The angle is: New studies are showing that rising world temperatures are drying out normally waterlogged forests and that these massive tropical rainforests and northern pine forests will go up in forest fires so massive that the smoke will begin to pollute the atmosphere. The studies said that in the 1990s more than twice as many acres burned in wildfires as in the 1960s...and that this may eliminate one of earth's resources for absorbing carbon dioxide.

One actuality is with Martin Forester, of the environmental team at the U.S. Department of Agriculture, who says that the northern forests of Canada and the United States may burn in forest fires. You have another bite with Thomas Fishburne, an oceanography professor at Texas A & M University, who said he didn't originally believe in global warming but now is a believer. And you have an actuality with Thomas Belchem, of the Northern States Industrial Council, who doesn't believe that global warming exists. Use the bites in any order you wish. Write the tracks around them. You will need four tracks.

Researcher Martin Forester :08
"It is underrepresented in the public consciousness and in the scientific attention it has gotten."

Professor Thomas Fishburne :13
"If it acts like a duck, walks like a duck, and quacks like a duck, you say it is a duck. This is 95 percent duck."

Thomas Belcham :10
"Scientists have yet to prove that the recent temperature increases are anything out of the ordinary."

CHAPTER SUMMARY

Remotes, voicers, Q-&-As, and wraps are the formats used by radio reporters in the field. Remotes are live, but voicers and wraps use a reporter's recorded narration segment called a track. Wraps, short for wraparounds, also use recorded interview segments called actualities.

These different report formats can use the narrative models discussed in Chapter 7.

Television: Writing to Stills and CGs

CHAPTER PREVIEW

To work for television news, a journalist must not only be a deft researcher and skilled writer, but also have mastered some elements of screen design, documentary video, and the interplay of words and recorded video frames and images.

This chapter deals with the combination of spoken words and still visuals on the television screen. TV newswriters often compose and reference static visuals and computer-generated graphics that are added electronically to the visual portion of the newscast. These visuals include over-the-shoulder topic boxes, partial screen CGs, lower-third CGs, and full-screen graphics, which include full-screen CGs, and maps, quotes, and illustrations. To make these visuals effective, correct referencing of the text to the visuals is crucial.

GLOSSARY

ANIMATION   A series of graphic screen pages played in succession to give the impression of sequential movement.

CG or FONT   Also often called a *title, key, lower-third key,* or *super,* this refers to computer-generated letters and numbers that either are superimposed over a picture or make up the entire screen over a colored background.

COPY BLOCK   In a television news script, the right half of the page that contains the words to be read by the newscaster. Quite often, this copy block is very narrow and exists between two lines on the page that show the limits of the teleprompter pickup.

OTS   For "over-the-shoulder." This refers to topic boxes keyed into the corner of the screen, boxes that often include CGs to add information.

PAGE   Each still picture that is called up from a computer or still store with visuals, CGs, or composites is always on a separate page of memory in those machines. Therefore, the entire individual screen is called a page and is usually identified by its numerical location within the machines. Also called a *screen.*

PRODUCTION CUES Script markings in the director's column that indicate places where there is a camera change or where to insert video or graphics.

REVEAL A sequence of CG pages that, when played in succession, give the impression that lines of copy are being added one at a time.

STILL STORE An electronic memory unit for storing single screens.

TOPIC BOX or BOX Generic identifiers usually placed in a box format to the newscaster's left or right. These usually remain in view throughout the story. Also called squeezes or frames.

VISUALS AS TOOLS

Writers use words, but television newswriters use words, visuals, videotape, and the combination of words and visuals to tell stories.

Anytime a graphic appears on the screen, it is a disorienting change from the picture already there. Newswriters, although not trained as graphic artists, must assist in the screen design and must be aware of the graphic's duration and placement in a series of visuals. Working with the computer graphics artist will help. More fundamental, however, are the following suggestions when working with visuals.

1. *Always reference the graphic.* This means that the copy, in some way, should explain the change in visuals. This is vitally important in the switch from the news studio image to a full screen visual or videotape, or during sequence changes on the videotape.

2. *Let the visuals tell some of the story.* For this, the writer must evaluate the visual in two ways. First, does the visual have such a powerful impact, as in the case of an air crash, that the pictures draw the viewer's attention from the narration? Second, can the visual provide simple story information that will not have to be put in the copy, such as the size of a crowd at a parade? New TV newswriters tend to waste time by describing what the audience can see and by adding excessive narration to situations in which the visual and the ambient sound provide details the audience can already see.

3. *Explain rather than describe the graphic.* The narration that accompanies the graphic should not describe the television screen but should talk about the situation or events the pictures represent.

4. *Design the graphic first, then write the story.* Graphics should not be added as afterthoughts. The writer must intend to write the story around the graphic. To do this, it is necessary to design the graphic first.

   Few of us are trained graphic artists; however, it is a good idea to sketch out what you want and then let the artist flesh out the details. If you have a story about a plane crash, then be certain to tell the artist what kind of plane (airliner or private plane) and other details that might be important. Also tell the artist if you are planning to have any CG title on the screen with the visual. With this information set, you can then design the story.

Although these four rules are being introduced in a chapter on still visuals, they apply to all visual work, including videotape and computer-generated graphics and animation.

PARTIAL SCREEN GRAPHICS

These are graphics that appear while the newscaster's face remains on the screen. The most common example is the OTS topic box in the corner of the screen. CGs, which are numbers or words for identification and informational purposes, are also used.

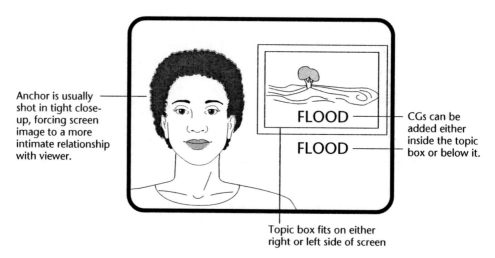

Anchor is usually shot in tight close-up, forcing screen image to a more intimate relationship with viewer.

FLOOD

FLOOD

CGs can be added either inside the topic box or below it.

Topic box fits on either right or left side of screen

FIGURE 9.1
Partial screen graphic.

OTS Topic Boxes

Over-the-shoulder (OTS) topic boxes have been the subject of intense study. Some researchers say this theme identifier in the corner of the screen has a powerful effect on the viewer. Improperly designed boxes may leave a wrong impression, no matter what the copy says. For example, if the story is a fire and the topic box incorrectly says "ARSON," viewers may still think the fire's cause is arson whether or not the copy confirms it.

Although topic boxes are constructed and inserted in many ways, the most common of them is to freeze a page of graphics on a still store page and shrink that in a control room switcher before it is keyed into the picture. Most all systems now use digital still store and computer-generated graphics techniques to compose topic boxes. Pre-production sessions can tie CG titles to topic pictures already in an electronic slide file. This allows great flexibility in changing or updating the OTS topic boxes.

An example could be the story of a military clash along the Serbian border. When the artist and the writer agree on the content, the pre-production producer gets the assignment. A map of the area is called up and frozen on the screen. The words "BORDER CLASH" are generated in the CG, and then keyed over the map. The composite graphic is then saved on a still store page. Later, in the newscast, the director calls for the page to be keyed in the screen corner by using a pre-set effect.

Changes in the topic box can be used to add information as the story progresses. Figure 9.2 provides an example of the changes that can be made to reference different ideas and visuals. Caution: this example is condensed to illustrate this point. A producer or writer would not call for so many changes within a single story.

SAN DIEGO RESIDENTS
THIS SUMMER WILL
HAVE SOME NEW PLACES
TO SPEND A LAZY
AFTERNOON.

THE STATE PARKS
SERVICE WILL REBUILD
THE ENCINITAS BEACH
FISHING PIER...
DAMAGED LAST WINTER
DURING HIGH TIDES
AND STORMS.

THE PIER HAS BEEN
CLOSED FOR SIX
MONTHS.

THE PARKS AGENCY
WILL ALSO FINISH UP
TWO BACK COUNTRY
HIKING AREAS NEAR
FISHBECK LAKE. EACH
HAS 200 CAMPSITES AND
BOAT LAUNCHING
FACILITIES.

THESE AREAS SHOULD
BE READY BY JUNE FIRST.

FOR RESERVATIONS...
CALL THE PARK SERVICE
AT 898-2227... THAT'S
8-9-8-2-2-2-7.

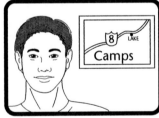

FIGURE 9.2
Changes in the topic box.

Don't rely too heavily on an unrealistic number of graphics. The artists and directors who do the pre-production composite work may not have enough time to prepare everything. In such a case, you would have to drop the topic boxes at the last minute, and possibly rewrite the story. Know the production realities of your station. Always ask the producer or editor what other graphics are being planned for this newscast. It may save you a lot of trouble later.

Partial CGs

Lower-third or corner CGs are electrically generated numbers and words that are superimposed over the studio picture or videotape to add information.

FIGURE 9.3
Lower-third CG.

Phone numbers are the most commonly added lower-third CG. If you provide phone numbers late in a story, alert your audience somewhere near the top. This will allow anyone who wants to write down the number to grab a pencil. Otherwise, these numbers go by so fast they are ineffective. Many stations repeat the info later in the newscast.

FIGURE 9.4
Demonstration of corner CGs.

How Long Should the CG Be On?

This has a lot to do with the complexity of the screen, the narration, and how the CG fits into the flow of other graphics.

A screen with words and numbers should be on long enough to read it aloud twice. That's the minimum. There is no set maximum, but you certainly don't want to leave something on the screen beyond the time that your narration has switched to another angle or topic.

FULL-SCREEN VISUALS

A full-screen visual is any that completely takes over the screen, causing the picture of the newscaster to disappear. This is a radical dislocation of the viewer's visual attention and requires care in use. A full-screen visual can be used in four ways:

1. as a CG to display facts

2. as a pre-produced composite with a videotape freeze-frame to display a quote

3. as a graphic composed by an artist for illustration

4. as a freeze-frame or still photograph

These uses are expanded upon in the following sections.

Using a CG To Display Facts

Generally, this is a full-screen graphic with words and numbers to support the copy. It may be all electronically generated or a composite with the words and numbers placed over a graphic. Although a news artist may complete the graphic design, it is the writer who must select what information goes on the screen.

Here are some rules to help you design screens:

- Use no more than five horizontal lines of copy. Otherwise, it gets too crowded and hard to read.

- Try to limit the letter count across the screen to 15. This will allow for a typeface that is large enough to read easily.

- A screen should be able to stand alone. It should have a title that is concise but understandable. Sometimes it takes a great deal of effort to devise a good title.

- Know the capabilities of the computer graphics machines. Most can place bands of different colored backgrounds on the screen. Quite often, it helps to use one color background with the title and one with the information. It is also simple to color the letters, but you want to avoid too many colors in the makeup.

The process of building a screen, shown in Figure 9.5, is simple.

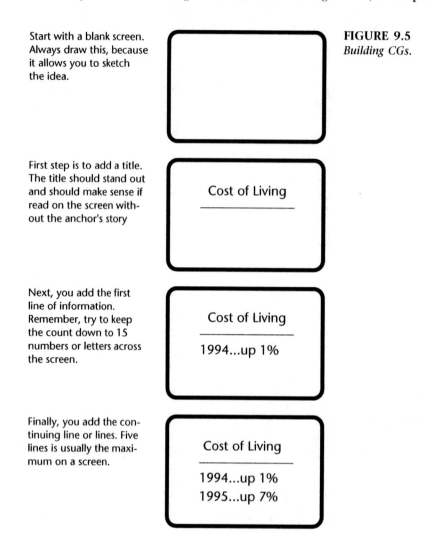

Start with a blank screen. Always draw this, because it allows you to sketch the idea.

First step is to add a title. The title should stand out and should make sense if read on the screen without the anchor's story

Next, you add the first line of information. Remember, try to keep the count down to 15 numbers or letters across the screen.

Finally, you add the continuing line or lines. Five lines is usually the maximum on a screen.

FIGURE 9.5
Building CGs.

Cost of Living

Cost of Living
_____
1994...up 1%

Cost of Living
_____
1994...up 1%
1995...up 7%

Indicating CG Position in the Script. It is very important to add a production cue to tell the director exactly when you want the full CG to appear and when you want to return to the newscaster's face. Although newsroom styles differ, it is also beneficial to write the information into the news prompter copy block, giving the anchor a clue as to where the audience attention lies. Figure 9.6 gives an example of a script with the graphic.

At the time that the midsection of the story was read, the full CG was on the screen. Notice how the director and anchor both get clear information about where the CG goes. Also notice that the CG supports the facts and is complementary, rather then being a literal copy of the words read on the screen.

```
_____ O/C              REPUBLICAN MARVIN
                          FOOTE SCORED AN UPSET
                          VICTORY IN SAN MATEO'S
                          16TH DISTRICT ELECTION
                          YESTERDAY.

FULL CG                   (full CG)
                          DEMOCRAT BILL BAHR
  ┌─────────────────┐     TRAILED FROM THE
  │   16th District │     START...AND WHEN THE
  │   ───────────   │     FINAL RESULTS WERE IN...
  │ Foote (R) 12,345│     BAHR WAS SO FAR BEHIND
  │ Bahr (D) 6,215  │     THAT POLITICAL
  └─────────────────┘     OBSERVERS ARE CALLING
                          IT A LANDSLIDE.

_____ O/C              (live)
                          FOOTE'S VICTORY IS THE
                          FIRST IN 30-YEARS FOR A
                          REPUBLICAN IN THE
                          TRI-CITIES AREA.
```

FIGURE 9.6
Using a full CG to complement a script.

Full-Screen Graphics

For this exercise, design a graphic or graphics to present the data. Then write a story complete with the correct instructions indicating where the graphic or graphics should go.

Situation

The federal government's Office of Economic Statistics in the Department of Commerce has just released a report showing the nation's inflation rate rose almost 2 percent last month.

The report also lists the inflationary price boosts for different areas of the country, including the Steeltown Metropolitan Area. There, inflation last month went up 1.2 percent. The price of all foods was up 2 percent, the price of gasoline up 4 cents a gallon to $1.85, and the price of most new clothing was up 3 percent. The cost of housing was up 6 percent. Durable goods held steady.

The Reveal   The reveal is a very effective use of successive full-screen CGs. In this case, you design a foundation or base page and then progressive additions that, when played in succession, make it seem that you are revealing information a line at a time.

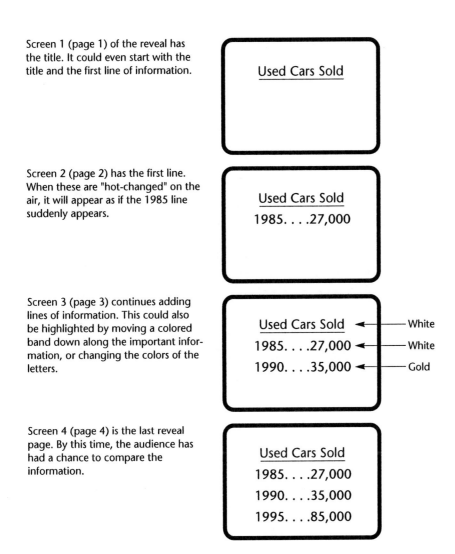

Screen 1 (page 1) of the reveal has the title. It could even start with the title and the first line of information.

Screen 2 (page 2) has the first line. When these are "hot-changed" on the air, it will appear as if the 1985 line suddenly appears.

Screen 3 (page 3) continues adding lines of information. This could also be highlighted by moving a colored band down along the important information, or changing the colors of the letters.

Screen 4 (page 4) is the last reveal page. By this time, the audience has had a chance to compare the information.

FIGURE 9.7
Building a reveal.

Using a Pre-produced Composite to Display a Quote

The combination of a freeze-frame from video and a character-generated quote fragment can have a strong effect on the viewer. Such a composite is usually made up in a pre-production session and recorded either in a single-page still store or as a visual freeze-frame on rolling videotape.

It is also important that this composite be inserted and taken out at exactly the proper moments in the story narrative. If the writer fails to add the correct production cues, and the director fails to intuitively figure out where it goes, then the effect will be to muddy the waters, rather than making them clear. See Figure 9.8 for an example.

The standard composite is the newsmaker's head in a freeze-frame compressed into a smaller window with a CG identifier and the words from the quote.

SMITH
"...a dangerous man."

FIGURE 9.8
Two composites, one showing a common problem.

Sometimes the artist may suggest putting both faces on the screen. This makes it difficult for the viewer to determine who is saying what about whom.

SMITH   HORNE
"...a dangerous man."

((EXERCISE 9-B))

A Composite for a Quote

For this exercise, design a composite picture and quote fragment to go with the story. You should be careful to make the design clear and to position the composite within the story so it has an effect. Also write the story (:30), complete with the correct instructions to the director.

Situation

School board president Randolph Erlich has been trying to get rid of a superintendent who is a constant critic of Erlich's management style. Now it looks as though Erlich has a cause. Today he announced that superintendent Roland Mowers will be investigated on allegations of "inappropriate conduct" towards minor schoolchildren.

Board president Erlich said that the conduct had to do with criminal child abuse charges and that he wouldn't say anything more. He said the district attorney's office is investigating.

Mowers is on vacation in the Bahamas and was unable to be reached for comment. You check, and your videotape library has good shots of each of the persons involved.

Using a Full Graphic or Animation for Illustration

Full graphics are most commonly used for diagrams illustrating a process or maps. In this case, the newswriter should sketch out a design for the artist and then meet with the artist before the story is written. If an animation is planned, the newswriter should suggest how the motion should look and let the artist handle the aesthetics of composition. On most occasions, the artist will offer advice about the design, simplifying it or changing its scale, which could affect the words chosen to accompany the graphic.

Simplicity is a key. Reduce the information in the graphic as much as possible, using only what is needed for the viewer to recognize the graphic quickly. The script instructions for this graphic are the same as for the full CG.

(((EXERCISE 9-C)))

Use a Full Graphic for Illustration

For this exercise, design a map to use in presentation of the data. Use only as much information on the map as is needed. Then write a story (:30) with the correct instructions indicating where the map should go.

Situation

Hurricane Danny is heading for the East Coast of the United States. It's considered a dangerous hurricane, and the winds are now 120 miles per hour. It is 300 miles off the Florida coast, due east of Cuba, and is moving at 15 miles per hour along a projected path that will take it over land somewhere in Florida. Two scenarios for landfall are predicted, depending on how the steering winds change. It could either hit well north of Miami or just south, in the same place where Hurricane Andrew struck in 1992, causing billions of dollars worth of damage.

You can make up maps, or use the computer animation from the weather bureau. It is a series of four satellite maps showing the hurricane's location up to the present spot.

Using a Still Photo or Freeze-Frame

Using a still or freeze-frame requires no additional skills. In either case, the writer should study the picture to evaluate what the viewer will get out of it. The picture tells part of the story. If someone in the picture is smiling, it is unnecessary for the writer to mention smiling. It is evident that this is going on. In this case rule 3, given at the beginning of this chapter, is very important: Explain, rather than describe, the graphic.

Another consideration will be the placement of the picture. Quite often, producers like the picture at the top of the story. Again, this will require the writer to think like a viewer: What needs immediate explanation? How long should the picture be there? Trial and error usually is the path to solving these questions.

CHAPTER SUMMARY

Switching from the straight-on shot of the anchor to a partial or full-screen visual is disorienting for the viewer. Therefore, the writer must reference the visual, let the visual tell some of the story, and explain rather than describe what's on the screen.

There are both partial visuals, inserted over-the-shoulder, beside, below, or across the newscaster, and full-screen visuals that replace the picture of the newscaster. A composite visual can combine a freeze-frame of tape with a CG quote to add effect to the narrative. Animation and still freeze-frames of videotape can also be useful full-screen graphic techniques.

Designing screens should be a collaborative effort with the news artist. The newswriter must direct what editorial material should be on the screen and in what order it should go, and the artist will carry out the design.

10

TV: Writing the
VO and the VO/SOT

CHAPTER PREVIEW

The *VO* or *voice over* story and the *VO/SOT* or *voice over into sound on tape* are heavily used in broadcast news and are a writer's routine assignment in television. In the VO, the anchor reads the copy from the studio and videotape is used for a portion of the story visuals. The writer must be aware of the sequence and continuity of videotape images, and how to relate these images to the story in the most effective manner. The VO/SOT form adds a soundbite to the VO story but also complicates the design of the script. This form can be extended to the VO/SOT/VO/SOT/VO and beyond.

GLOSSARY

B-ROLL   A term for additional pictures, used for illustration and explanation, which are not on the same tape as the principal audio narration or interview.

CLOSEUP (CU)   An intimate camera shot, it usually encloses the face with some room between the image and the frame's border. An extreme close up (ECU) will cut off the hairline and the chin and is used for emotional moments; however, it is an uncomfortable shot and should be used sparingly, if at all.

CONTINUITY   The orderly flow of images for any location, action, or time period in a videotape sequence.

COVER   (In picture stories) A collection of video that supports a certain amount of narration in a story. Used as a noun (Do we have enough cover?) or a verb (Cover that part of the narration).

COVER   (in the introduction to an SOT) Routine production shots of an interviewee doing nonspecific daily tasks such as answering phones, walking down hallways, and the like.

CUTAWAYS   Short (:01 to :03) shots inserted into an interview sequence to draw the point of view away from the single closeup shot. These shots are usually reverse angle or medium shots and allow a videotape editor to compress an interview during the editing process.

ESTABLISHING SHOT (ES)   First visual in a sequence. It orients the viewers to a new location or theme. In the past, it was usually only a wide shot (WS), but now any shot, whether wide (WS), medium (MS), or closeup (CU) will do if it offers immediate identification for the upcoming sequence.

GENERIC VISUALS   More specific to a particular story than wallpaper video, these illustrate a story but are timeless and not tied to any specific current event. An example would be shots of aspirin bottles for a story on dangers of aspirin. File tape also can be an example of generic visuals. Although valuable at times, generic visuals are often overused.

JUMP CUT   A sudden visual jerk in the image at the edit point of two shots that have very similar but not identical pictures. An example would be the joining of two closeups of the same person when each has the face in different portions of the frame. A jump cut could also occur if the person was wearing glasses in one shot but not the other. Two medium shots of the same subject might jump if taken from the same spot.

POINT-OF-VIEW SHOTS (POV)   A camera angle in which the lens appears to be an eye of a person watching the action. An example would be shots out the front window of a car during a sequence picturing someone driving a car. As with the reaction shot, inserting a POV shot in a sequence allows other cuts to take place that might have been awkward.

REACTION SHOTS   Closeups (CUs) or medium shots (MSs) of people or crowds who are spectators to an event in question. Inserting this reaction shot allows the editor to compress the action, change point of view, join two shots that otherwise would have been a jump cut.

SEQUENCE   A series of videotape shots that tells the story of a single action, event, or time period. The sequence usually intercuts different focal length shots, such as closeups (CUs), medium shots (MSs), and wide shots (WSs), to achieve variety.

UPCUT   An error in transition that happens when the end of the audio currently being played conflicts with the beginning of the audio from the next source. This is usually the result of an error in timing; however, it forces the director or engineer on the audio board to make a sudden choice about which audio will play. If the upcut is severe, it often results in a situation where one audio portion will not make much sense.

VO or VOICE OVER   A television news story format that uses a studio newscaster for picture and audio but inserts videotape for visuals during a portion of the story.

VO/SOT   A commonly used story format in television news that combines a studio voice over segment with a soundbite. This can also be expanded to a VO/SOT/VO or even a VO/SOT/VO/SOT/VO.

WALLPAPER VIDEO   Use of random unconnected shots out of sequence as cover for the narration.

THE VO

If you've already practiced conversational writing, careful journalistic editing, and the use of still visuals, then you are ready for the next step—mastering the complex interrelationships of the visual medium. Former NBC News president Reuven Frank always stressed that television news was photojournalism and that reporters and writers needed to know how to use moving visuals. The least complex text and video relationship is the VO.

The VO or voice over story is a television workhorse, one of the four basic formats. It is generally a brief story, ranging from :20 to :45 of total story time. In some commercial local newscasts, used alone or in combinations called wraps, it might account for up to 10 of the stories in a single newscast.

Visual Sequences

When you are planning a VO, you have to write it around the video sequences that make up the visual summary of the event. A sequence is a series of related and varied shots that tells the story of a single event, location, or time period. Sequences are composed of many shots including the WS, MS, CU, and reverse shots, point-of-view shots, high-angle and low-angle shots, shots with action in them, and shots with camera movement or lens movement (*pans* or *tilts*). In some circumstances, a sequence may be a single :20 shot with a lot of action or five carefully selected shots that last :10. Sometimes sequences are combined to form a short VO story. Even VO stories with a tape TRT (total running time) of :20 might have three sequences within that short time period.

Sequences are the backbone of visual presentation and anyone wishing to do television news work should understand there is a range in quality of sequences.

The least effective use of video is called wallpaper, using random nonrelated but thematically similar shots. For instance, in a story about contaminated soda cans being recalled, wallpaper would be random, unconnected shots of any soda cans, delivery trucks, or supermarkets.

A better use, but not the optimum, is called generic video, which includes random shots related to this individual story but telling no particular story. In our soda recall story, this might be various pictures of the soda cans in question.

An even better use is called B-roll, where the pictures are cut literally to illustrate the narration, but still are not in a sequence.

Finally, the strongest possible video is a sequence that illustrates the narration, but also tells a story in pictures. This is accomplished by intercutting WSs, MSs, and CUs, and all the other shots. At this point in the VO, the narration could stop and the tape sound would carry the story.

Rules for Sequences

As you can see, sequences are the most sought after field visuals. These sequences are usually constructed from shots collected for that purpose. There are certain rules worth remembering when editing sequence shots.

1. *Begin with the best establishing shot (ES) you can find.* Most broadcast news sequences are short, about three or four shots, and go by quickly. For that reason, choose your best video for your sequence opener. This establishing shot should either give perspective or should immediately identify the topic for viewers. The traditional establisher is the wide shot, but television's intimate screen has allowed others also to serve that purpose. Relationship shots, in which the shooter has placed two major elements of the story (for example, the trainer and the new seeing eye dogs, the new development and the unused lot ready for expansion, and so on) are excellent as establishing shots.

2. *Maintain continuity.* Most viewers can sense when your shots are out of chronological order. If the story is about an event, it is easy to follow the passage of time. The protestors gathered, they conferred, they marched toward the police, the police watched, the protestors pushed the police, the police pushed back, the protestors retreated. If the shots were out of order, the story would lack continuity. There are some major continuities to watch for:

   Location. The site where the particular event takes place. If a demonstration happened in three locations—a park, a downtown street, and in front of city hall—then shots for each must be separate from the others.

   Time. If a candidate comes to town, then your visual story, if it isn't taking a special angle, should follow the schedule. Start with the arrival at the airport, then the motorcade, the city hall greeting, the meetings with party workers, the fund-raising dinner, and finally the return to the airport.

   Action. If you are telling the story of a price rise for frozen orange juice, and you are using pictures from the processing plant, then the shots should be arranged in the order the processing takes place. The oranges arrive by truck, are dumped onto a belt, sized, sliced, squeezed, the juice flows down plastic pipes, and so on.

3. *Alternate WS, MS, & CUs to provide variety.* These shots show the placement of the camera. Not only should you alternate focal lengths, but you should also alternate angles, using shots from different perspectives to complete a sequence. This will give the videotape editor a variety of shots and prevent the editor from considering jump cuts.

4. *Vary shot length.* A sequence that is a series of still :03 shots becomes very predictable. An exciting event can be made dull by predictable shots.

5. *Insert reaction and point-of-view shots to help condense sequences.* A reaction shot is a CU of a face in the crowd, such as a concerned parent watching the rescue of a child. After three shots of someone at a podium, a POV (point-of-view) shot reverses the direction to let the audience sample what the speaker is seeing. These shots are vital to editing. Be certain that the shooter provides these shots.

Twin Tower Concept

The writer must think of the VO as a dual story. Veteran television reporter and newswriter Bill Rukeyser used to teach interns and junior writers about the VO by having them imagine it as two towers constructed at the same time: one is the narration from the studio and the other is the picture story that runs opposite it. Although the edited videotape is inserted over the newscaster's picture during the newscast, both the narration and the visuals should be able to stand alone. In fact, if a VO is well written, the narration should be credible even if the videotape doesn't run. In a like manner, the videotape, if shown without narration, should make some sense and contain many of the elements of the story.

Reviewing Rules for Visuals

Let's review three of the rules for working with visuals that were given in Chapter 9, and let's now add a new fourth one.

1. *Always reference the visual.* For the viewer, each screen change from studio visuals to videotape and back is a crucial moment. Although the newscaster's face is familiar, the videotape scenes generally are not. Therefore, it is absolutely necessary that you are talking about what's seen in the tape at the same time as the viewer sees the first frames.

2. *Let the visuals tell some of the story.* Look at the videotape without any narration. It should be telling a story and passing along information. You don't need to say the traffic was heavy if the viewer can see the street was busy.

   On the same note, there might be a point of effective ambient, or natural, sound where you can write a "pause" notation into the copy block. In this case, your video with its synch SOT brought up should be enough to convey the meaning without any narration at all. You, the writer, must judge how long to pause. If needed, you can add the time to the notation (pause :03), or you can go over the script with the newscaster and allow him or her to set the correct duration of the pause.

3. *Explain rather than describe.* The rule is to talk about but not to describe exactly what the viewers are seeing. For a story on a barn, don't say it is red because they can see that; instead, mention its history, that it was used as a dairy, and so on. Avoid the phrase "as you see here."

4. *Watch out for sensationalism.* Sensationalism means different things to different people. It can be defined, however, as the use of visuals to thrill and amaze your audience. When you are working with any photojournalism, including VOs, it is easy to pick out a sensational moment and highlight that, giving your viewers a misleading impression about events that day.

   An example might occur during the coverage of a parade. For two or three hours, nothing much happens, except for bands, floats, and reax shots of little kids. Then someone throws an empty bottle at one of the floats and a scuffle breaks out as security guards wrestle with the bottle tosser. Back at the station, your producer gives you :30 total for the story and expects at least :20 of videotape. If you use the bottle thrower, the sequence of shots necessary to explain it will take almost all of the :20. What do you do? If you use it, you might leave the impression that the entire parade was a melee. If you don't, are you ignoring an important or unusual event that did happen so you can portray the parade as peaceful? Discuss this in class.

What Kind of Shots Are Best for VOs?

We assume that you are familiar with the special points of writing for spoken news. Now we are introducing you to a new language, the unique grammar of film. Having some pictures—any pictures—is not necessarily the answer. Finding the best use of video sequences is the goal. Here are some suggestions for selecting from raw material:

- *Use shots with people rather than empty shots.* More often than not, although broadcast stories generally are about people, you have to show buildings, laboratories, offices, parking lots, parks, and so on. In these cases, it is better to have people in them than a deserted landscape.

- *Use action rather than still shots.* In most cases, where it doesn't distort the summary of a story, shots with action are preferable to shots without. If you are showing the front of a company's building, choose a shot with people going in and out the front door rather than the same shot with people standing still. This rule applies only when the selection of the shot does not alter the impression a viewer may get about the amount of activity during an event.

- *Use closeups rather than wide shots.* The television screen is small and people often sit a great distance from it. It is very hard to see tiny detail. Select closeup shots when possible.

- *Use simple rather than complex shots.* It's much easier to write stories about shots that focus on one or two items, rather than those jammed with information. Look for unified themes in shots.

- *Use shots with restrained camera movement.* Camera movement is the use of pans (side-to-side), zooms (in-and-out), tilts (up-and-down), racking focus (going in and out of focus), and walking shots. Although a little camera movement is okay at times, a sequence where five out of six shots have camera movement is generally overdone and intrusive to the topic the story is attempting to report. Also, shots with camera movement require that the entire movement be used in the editing. Some of these shots, especially the pan, can be :20 long.

- *Use shots with ambient sound.* Sound is integral to every moment of life. Sounds aid our learning processes. Running silent video cheats the viewers of the ambience that helps us gather information from the videotape.

- *Avoid generic visuals.* Generic visuals refer to videotape not shot for this story but related to the story in a general and timeless way. Quite often file tape is used generically and, in many cases, file tape requires extra explanation to orient the viewers to what they are seeing.

Steps to the VO Story

In the best of all worlds, untouched by deadline pressure or videotape editing availability, there is a suggested order for writing a VO: (a) research the story; (b) design the story; (c) review the videotape; and (d) write the story.

Research the Story. First, determine from the research what will be important in the story. Establish this as if there weren't going to be any visuals. Be ready to change if your supporting visuals dictate a change.

Design the Story. Second, consult with the producer about the TST (total story time) and placement of the videotape within your story. Since the total story times of VOs may run up to 1:00, it is important to see what the newscast producer has planned for the length of the story.

Both the total story time and placement of the videotape within the VO will force changes in the story design. There are several different video placements. Most VO stories begin and end with on-camera segments in the studio, and the video is inserted in the story's midsection. But a VO might also begin in the studio and end in video or even open with video off the top and end in on-camera in the studio.

In the story that follows, which has a middle placement, you can see how the words "A few buildings..." form the reference for the pictures of fallen buildings.

```
_____O/C       ANOTHER DEADLY DISASTER
                  IN THE MEDITERRANEAN
                  YESTERDAY.

VIDEO VO                  (vo)
                  A FEW BUILDINGS ARE ALL
                  THAT ARE LEFT IN GRIMALDI...
                  SARDINIA...AFTER A MAJOR
                  EARTHQUAKE STRUCK THE
                  FARMING CENTER.
                      RESCUE CREWS ARE STILL
                  HUNTING THROUGH
```

COLLAPSED APARTMENT
BUILDINGS AND STORES.

AT ONE TIME...IT WAS
FEARED THE DEATH TOLL
WOULD REACH 45...BUT NOW
ONLY SEVEN ARE CONFIRMED
DEAD.

_____O/C   (live)

OFFICIALS SAY MOST OF THE
BUILDINGS FELL IN A PART OF
TOWN BUILT OVER AN OLD
LAKE BED.

What would happen, though, if you had the same story information but the only pictures available are of the hospital? Because video forces the writer's hand, the story must be redesigned. The script calls for the VO in the middle position, with the story beginning and ending in the studio. You'll have to change the information in the story to match the video you have.

_____O/C   (live)

A FEW BUILDINGS ARE ALL
THAT ARE LEFT IN
GRIMALDI...SARDINIA...AFTER A
MAJOR EARTHQUAKE HIT THE
FARMING CENTER ON
MONDAY.

RESCUE CREWS ARE STILL
SEARCHING THROUGH FALLEN
BUILDINGS AND STORES.

VIDEO VO   (vo)

DOCTORS AT NEARBY
MELEANIA HOSPITAL SAY THE
DEATH TOLL IS NOW SEVEN.

TODAY OFFICIALS APPEALED
FOR MEDICINES AND
BANDAGES...SAYING THE
SUPPLY AT THE TOWN'S SMALL
TRT :10   HOSPITAL IS RUNNING OUT.

_____O/C   (live)

INTERNATIONAL RELIEF
SUPPLIES HAVEN'T REACHED
THE DISASTER AREA
YET...BECAUSE THE QUAKE
DESTROYED TOO MANY ROADS
AND BRIDGES.

All of this reinforces our rule: The VO forces the design.

In Figure 10.1, you can see two examples of another VO story, but with different videotape, again showing how the writer must consider what pictures are available. Guess what the video is in each.

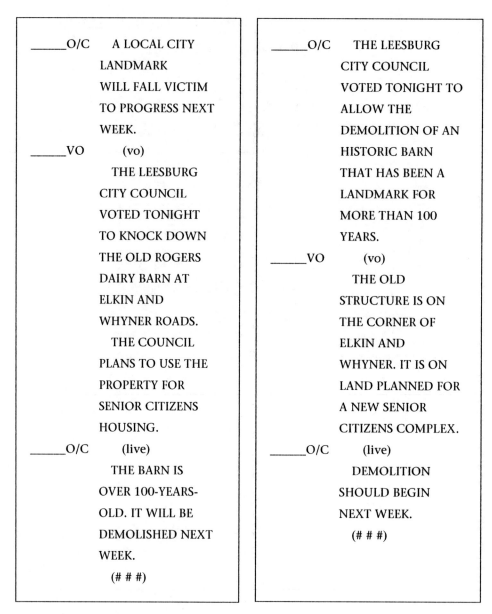

_____O/C   A LOCAL CITY
             LANDMARK
             WILL FALL VICTIM
             TO PROGRESS NEXT
             WEEK.

_____VO   (vo)
             THE LEESBURG
             CITY COUNCIL
             VOTED TONIGHT
             TO KNOCK DOWN
             THE OLD ROGERS
             DAIRY BARN AT
             ELKIN AND
             WHYNER ROADS.
               THE COUNCIL
             PLANS TO USE THE
             PROPERTY FOR
             SENIOR CITIZENS
             HOUSING.

_____O/C   (live)
             THE BARN IS
             OVER 100-YEARS-
             OLD. IT WILL BE
             DEMOLISHED NEXT
             WEEK.
               (# # #)

_____O/C   THE LEESBURG
             CITY COUNCIL
             VOTED TONIGHT TO
             ALLOW THE
             DEMOLITION OF AN
             HISTORIC BARN
             THAT HAS BEEN A
             LANDMARK FOR
             MORE THAN 100
             YEARS.

_____VO   (vo)
             THE OLD
             STRUCTURE IS ON
             THE CORNER OF
             ELKIN AND
             WHYNER. IT IS ON
             LAND PLANNED FOR
             A NEW SENIOR
             CITIZENS COMPLEX.

_____O/C   (live)
             DEMOLITION
             SHOULD BEGIN
             NEXT WEEK.
               (# # #)

FIGURE 10.1.
Two examples of the same VO story, but with different videotape.

Seeking Sequences

In this exercise, write down a list of sequences and a list of shots you would like on the raw field tape. Don't forget to specify WS, MS, or CUs. Then write stories for each situation. All stories are expected to be :35 with about :20 of VO in the normal position.

Situation 1

You have a story about shortages of electric power. The scant supply comes from the need to perform maintenance at power plants, and too many went off-line at the same time. State regulators are warning of rolling blackouts.

Situation 2

A local entrepreneur has started a business that buys baked goods and delivers them to your home. The company has a small office and warehouse next door to a major supermarket down at the Mar Vista Estates Shopping Center. Orders are taken over the phone, filled in the warehouse, and then driven by van to your door.

Situation 3

A local company has announced a new electric van for intercity commercial use. This has a revolutionary battery in it. They presented the van today at a news conference and allowed reporters to drive it.

Situation 4

Protestors say the federal government is not providing enough funding for AIDS research. The demonstrators chained themselves to the doors of the local federal offices.

Review the Videotape. The third step in writing a VO is to review the videotape. You might be using either a raw field tape or an edited videotape from the file library, off the network, or from a longer package. You might be lucky and find a well-edited one, and the sequences are the ones you need; or you may find your new story needs a slightly different angle or needs shots that aren't there. In any case, you'll have to write exactly to the length of the shots, something we'll practice later in this chapter.

If you are using raw field tape, you'll have to look for complete sequences and evaluate omissions. Log the tape and mentally group shots you think will make a sequence, then make a decision on the TRT (it generally is :15 to :20), and give the editor a detailed shot sheet with shot order and times on it.

This is difficult for the new television newswriter. What do you pick? Experience helps. If a good shooter gives you 10 minutes of good sequence material and you have to pick only shots that add up to :20, then you're set. But if a mediocre shooter gives you only about two minutes of possible shots, then it is much more critical that you pick right.

Write the Story. The fourth step in preparing a VO is to write the story. Now, you've got two main concerns. To begin with, you must arrange your information so that you reference the video exactly at the point where the tape is first seen. Also, you must write the news copy to match the exact reading speed of the newscaster, if you hope to have words and pictures match.

Referencing is important because weak or missing referencing will confuse the audience, killing any hope for comprehension or understanding. Referencing matches words and pictures. You must refer to the first visuals, even if done in an off-hand manner.

For example, if both of the stories in Figure 10.2 use the same visuals of a city council meeting, it's easy to see that the one on the left has very weak referencing of first words.

Learning to Write to the Time of Video

In certain situations, the writer must compose stories to match the times of edited video. It is hard to do. The longer the VO, the harder it gets.

Say you have an already edited dub of a VO from another source and the shots are too short to rearrange. It describes the meeting of some politicians. If the senator shows up at :08 and the county chairwoman at :12, you'll need to hit those times in your script. Or perhaps you are working on several stories under deadline with no time to recut the VO video after you've written the final script. The newsreader then must adjust his or her phrasing to hit the right times.

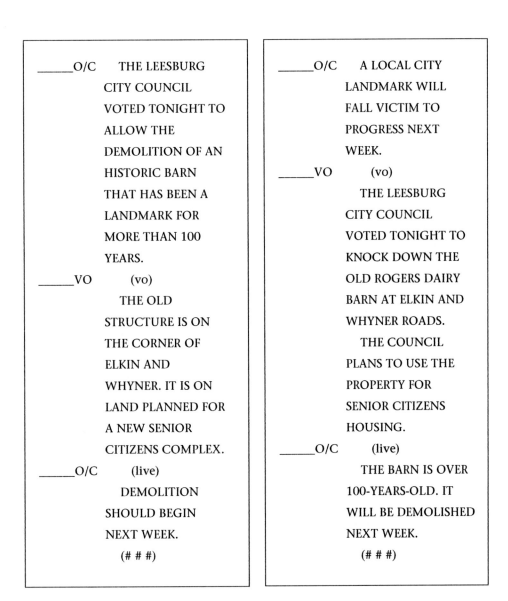

_____O/C   THE LEESBURG
CITY COUNCIL
VOTED TONIGHT TO
ALLOW THE
DEMOLITION OF AN
HISTORIC BARN
THAT HAS BEEN A
LANDMARK FOR
MORE THAN 100
YEARS.

_____VO   (vo)
THE OLD
STRUCTURE IS ON
THE CORNER OF
ELKIN AND
WHYNER. IT IS ON
LAND PLANNED FOR
A NEW SENIOR
CITIZENS COMPLEX.

_____O/C   (live)
DEMOLITION
SHOULD BEGIN
NEXT WEEK.

(# # #)

_____O/C   A LOCAL CITY
LANDMARK WILL
FALL VICTIM TO
PROGRESS NEXT
WEEK.

_____VO   (vo)
THE LEESBURG
CITY COUNCIL
VOTED TONIGHT TO
KNOCK DOWN THE
OLD ROGERS DAIRY
BARN AT ELKIN AND
WHYNER ROADS.
THE COUNCIL
PLANS TO USE THE
PROPERTY FOR
SENIOR CITIZENS
HOUSING.

_____O/C   (live)
THE BARN IS OVER
100-YEARS-OLD. IT
WILL BE DEMOLISHED
NEXT WEEK.

(# # #)

FIGURE 10.2
Two examples of VOs. Left, _VO with poor referencing;_ right, _one with better referencing._

Writing to Times

The following is a simple :30 VO, which begins and ends in the studio, with :20 of tape in the normal middle placement. The script you have below is only the VO portion of the script. We are trying to see if the time it takes to read the script matches the video shots you have selected. If it doesn't, adjust the script length by removing or adding words and phrases until the time matches the video cuts.

This is the shot list you gave to the videotape editor to cut the VO.

00:00-00:03 Shot of pandas arriving in truck

00:03-00:08 Reaction shot of kids watching

00:08-00:14 Zoo workers lift cage down and open it.

00:14-00:20 Zookeepers scratch pandas on head.

Now, make the timing work by editing the script, if need be.

_____VO   TWO SEMI TRUCKS BROUGHT THE CAGES WITH THE TINY CARGO. OFFICIALS SAID THE PRECAUTIONS ARE A SIGN OF HOW PRECIOUS THESE ANIMALS ARE.

      SCHOOLCHILDREN ON HAND TO WATCH THE ARRIVAL PUSHED CLOSER TO SEE THE TRAVEL WEARY ANIMALS WHO HAD COME FROM THE WASHINGTON ZOO.

      THESE GIANT PANDAS NORMALLY LIVE IN THE FORESTS OF WESTERN CHINA. THERE ARE ONLY 200 LEFT IN THE WILD AND ANOTHER 60 AT ZOOS AROUND THE WORLD. THE PANDAS LOOKED OUT OF PLACE IN THE OVERSIZED SHIPPING CAGES.

      BUT AFTER A FEW MINUTES...IT WAS OBVIOUS THE ZOOKEEPERS WERE GOOD AT CALMING THE TRAVELERS.

More Writing to Times

As in the previous exercise, adjust this script to make the time hit the references you think are needed. Again, you are using only the VO portion of the script.

This is the videotape rundown that went to the tape editor.

:04 WS of police watching demonstrators

:05 MS of demonstrators advancing up the capitol steps

:02 CU police put handcuffs on one demonstrator

:06 MS police take pictures of arrestees and put them in van

:05 WS line of police chases crowd down street

VO _____   (vo)
                    DEMONSTRATORS MET AT THE DOWNTOWN PLAZA PARK
                    AT NOON BEFORE THEY CONFRONTED POLICE ACROSS THE
                    STREET.
                    THE PROTESTORS HAD PRACTICED THEIR MOVES FOR
                    MONTHS...AND SHORTLY BEFORE NOON...THE FIRST WAVE
                    ADVANCED UP THE STEPS.
                    THEY WERE MET AT THE TOP BY POLICE...WHO PUSHED
                    THE DEMONSTRATORS BACK. BUT THEN THE CROWD
                    SURGED FORWARD AND SOME BEGAN TO LIE DOWN ON
                    THE TOP OF THE STEPS...BLOCKING ACCESS TO THE
                    DOORS.
                    POLICE THEN STARTED THE ARRESTS. OFFICERS SAY THEY
                    CITED AND RELEASED 70 DEMONSTRATORS. THE CITATIONS
                    CALL FOR AN APPEARANCE IN MUNICIPAL COURT NEXT
                    WEEK
                    AS THE PROTEST GREW SMALLER...SOME GROUPS BEGAN TO
                    RUN THROUGH DOWNTOWN TRAFFIC.

Choosing Shots

In this exercise, you are to make a :35 VO story out of the situation described below. The videotape in this story should run :20 and appears in the normal middle position with an on-camera open and close.

First, review the list of shots, choose the ones you would like used, then suggest the length of each shot and the order of the shots. Remember, you want a total of :20. Next, write the story using those shot lengths. Don't cheat by going back and changing the shot length after you have written the story. Get some practice in adjusting your script length.

Situation

You have a story about large pieces of sculpture being placed in four of Steeltown's parks. These are cast bronze pieces and the children are encouraged to climb on them and play with them. It is part of a program from a group called Art for People. The sculptures will be there for two weeks. The Art for People officials think this will introduce the kids to the beauty of lifesize sculptures. Most of the works are copies of Rodin's pieces.

Some critics are charging the statues will be vandalized.

You have the following raw tape shot list:

00:00-00:10	WS of park with empty playground
00:10-00:17	WS of park with some kids in playground
00:17-00:25	MS of kids climbing on sculpture
00:25-00:35	MS kids climb on standing man sculpture
00:35-00:40	CU of kids near head of statue
00:40-00:45	CU of kid near arm of statue
00:45-00:55	CU of kid—head pops out behind statue
00:55-01:05	MS kid pounds a baseball bat on sculpture

WRITING THE VO/SOT

The combination of a voice over segment with a soundbite is a heavily used but difficult-to-write format for television news. Often, the VO/SOT (pronounced "VOH-SOT") is extended to include another VO segment and is then called a VO/SOT/VO. The VO/SOT must be carefully structured, because it is tightly compressed and allows little time for expansive writing. It is also the story format that is most likely to have mishaps on the air.

The difficulties with the VO/SOT lie within its nature as a compromise between the VO, which can be done well in the studio, and the SOT, which is more easily handled in a reporter package.

Producers look to VO/SOTs for many reasons. A reporter package from an earlier newscast may need an update and the reporter cannot be found. Your own reporter may have shot part of a package but didn't have time to get enough visuals or other interviews. You have an interview by your own reporter but the extra visuals must come from file tape. You are drastically recutting a network piece and you cannot use the reporter's voicetrack. Sometimes your station photographers shoot a story alone, without a reporter, and the story must be assembled.

The solution is the VO/SOT. Because it is meant for the studio newscaster, total story time for a VO/SOT might run anywhere from :40 to 1:15, enough for a good VO but sometimes not enough to combine the VO with all that goes with the soundbite and with other nonvisual information in the story.

Time is not the only problem. Both the VO portion and the SOT may be strong enough to force the story design—but in different ways. Also, the soundbite will need :06 to :10 seconds of writeup, but this writeup must be accompanied by visuals because it will be located at the end of the VO segment.

Using Multiple Video Sources During the Newscast

Historically, the VO and the SOT were edited together onto one tape, causing problems if the anchor read too quickly (long silent gap) or too slowly (upcut and overriding of the bite). This problem was most severe if the VO was long—more than :20.

If two video source machines are available, it is easier to set up the VO on one and the SOT on another. The SOT portion is then rolled when the anchor gets to it and is not dependent on paced reading of the VO. In the example that follows, the SOT cassette would not roll until the anchor finished the VO copy block, whether or not the VO videotape had finished its TRT (total running time).

Here's a VO/SOT script with the tape in the normal position. Notice that the left side of the script gives the director production cues about where the sound comes up on the tape. This is often done in stations with separate editing sheets called *cutsheets*.

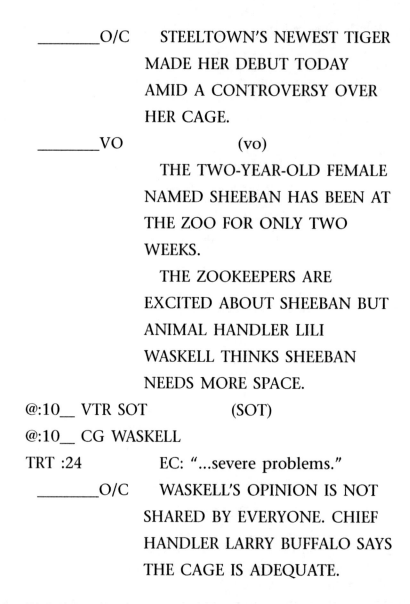

```
_____O/C      STEELTOWN'S NEWEST TIGER
                MADE HER DEBUT TODAY
                AMID A CONTROVERSY OVER
                HER CAGE.
_____VO                 (vo)
                THE TWO-YEAR-OLD FEMALE
                NAMED SHEEBAN HAS BEEN AT
                THE ZOO FOR ONLY TWO
                WEEKS.
                    THE ZOOKEEPERS ARE
                EXCITED ABOUT SHEEBAN BUT
                ANIMAL HANDLER LILI
                WASKELL THINKS SHEEBAN
                NEEDS MORE SPACE.
@:10__ VTR SOT            (SOT)
@:10__ CG WASKELL
TRT :24         EC: "...severe problems."
_____O/C      WASKELL'S OPINION IS NOT
                SHARED BY EVERYONE. CHIEF
                HANDLER LARRY BUFFALO SAYS
                THE CAGE IS ADEQUATE.
```

Using Cutaway Visuals to Cover the Writeup

Because the writeup text backs up into the VO, it must now have a visual component cover shot as well. That requires that, in the previous example, we see the zookeeper at exactly the same time you mention her name in the VO. This is usually accomplished by inserting the two-shot cutaway before the soundbite (SOT).

If the writeup is excessively long, in the area of :10, then you'll need to insert a sequence of cover shots leading up to the SOT. The classic is a closeup (CU) of the interviewee, then the two-shot, then the SOT. The CU is taken from a part of the interview where the zookeeper's mouth was closed and she was listening to your question, and the two-shot is a cutaway shot before or after the interview. In either case, both of these will be in the interview field tape.

However, they will be edited to become the second half of the VO. This is the progression of shots for the tiger story.

00:05 MS Tiger prowls cage

00:03 CU Tiger's face.

00:08 CU of Waskell (not speaking)

00:03 MS of Waskell and interviewer

00:14 SOT of Waskell.

Using Another VO or an On-Camera Tag

If you use the VO/SOT/VO, you can put additional information into the second VO portion. If the same anchor reads the next story, it's quite possible you won't need an on-camera tag.

If the story does not have an additional VO portion, the on-camera tag is always necessary before another story can be read. It's a good place to put information you didn't get a chance to use before the SOT, especially if that material is not visual, and it allows the viewer to re-establish contact with the voice that has been reading the VO/SOT before an anchor switch.

Any tag, whether in VO or not, completes the story. The SOT may be incomplete in telling the story and needs some perspective. The tag is also a place to paraphrase other comments from the SOT that bear on the story.

Writing a VO/SOT

For this exercise, write a VO/SOT/VO script that is :50 TST, including :10 of studio on-camera at the top and a :05 on-camera tag. In addition, you must select which shots you want put together to make up the :35 of video. You have VO from different sources.

Situation

The state highway department has announced it is going to rip up two miles of the Crosstown Highway for four weeks to repair certain bridges. They are going to divert traffic on another road two miles away. Merchants who own stores on the Crosstown Highway are furious. There will be no access to their businesses. They are hinting at a lawsuit to stop the repair work.

You have :30 of file VO from an accident last November that was caused by a crack in the roadway of Crosstown Highway. Several people were seriously injured. This includes:

:06   WS of accident scene

:02   CU of Crosstown Highway sign

:14   MS of a victim on stretcher being put into ambulance

:08   MS of tow truck driving off with one of the wrecks

You also have :30 of new video shot today by your crew.

:18   WS (3) of traffic on Crosstown Highway

:04   MS of exterior of Bob's Garden supply

:04   MS of the Bath Boutique

:04   MS of Glidden's Shell Station

You have an interview with Robert Belden, owner of Bob's Garden Supply. Plus, you have these cutaway interview shots.

:04 two-shot of reporter and Gelden

:08 MS of Gelden only (he's listening to question)

:04 CU of Gelden (he's listening to question)

And you have the following bite from the interview, which runs :14.

"Closing this road down makes no sense. How are we supposed to make money? With a little planning, they could only shut down one lane. This is the easy way out."

Breaking Down a Package to Write a VO/SOT

For this exercise, write a VO/SOT/VO script that is 1:05 TST, including :10 of studio on-camera at the top and a :05 on-camera tag. To do this, you must rework the following long package script on the donation of a $35,000 truck to the local county food bank. Remember to consider which video runs with which text.

(shots of truck pulling up to back of restaurant and workers helping load boxes of produce and cans onto the truck)

Track #1. "THE NEW REFRIGERATED TRUCK MADE ITS FIRST ROUNDS TODAY...PICKING UP EXCESS FOOD FROM 12 RESTAURANTS. THE TRUCK'S DRIVER...HENRY WILLIAMS...THINKS THE NEW STORAGE WILL HELP THE COUNTY'S HOMELESS."

    Bite #1. "We used to have to get this stuff to storage as soon as possible. Now we can go from source to source without the food spoiling...and this shortens our pickup times."

(shots of Williams in the cab, driving to warehouse, workers unloading the truck, a forklift, and workers sorting the contents into large blue plastic bins)

Track #2. "SHORTENING THE PICKUP TIME IS A BIG STEP FOR WILLIAMS. BY KEEPING THE TRUCK ON THE ROUTE, HE GETS THE FOOD BACK TO THE COUNTRY FOOD WAREHOUSE IN THE INDUSTRIAL PARK IN ONE TRIP. THE DAY'S HARVEST IS SORTED, REPACKAGED, AND SENT TO THE SIX COUNTY SOUP KITCHENS. COUNTY FOOD BANK DIRECTOR ELLEN STEPHENS THINKS THIS WILL IMPROVE THE FOOD QUALITY."

    Bite #2. "It can't help but taste better because it's fresher. Before the truck...we used to have to store it overnight and send it out the next day. Now it gets in and out in one day."

(shots of the truck pulling up and a worker using a hand dolly to roll boxes off the truck)

Track #3. "WORKERS AT THE ROGERS RELIEF FUND KITCHEN THINK THAT THE QUICK TURNAROUND IS WONDERFUL. AS THEY UNLOADED TODAY'S SUPPLIES...THEY PRAISED THE FUNDRAISING EFFORTS TO GET THE TRUCK."

    Bite #3. "It took a lot of work. The people behind this idea spent days and weeks hitting up people for help."

(continued)

(shots of the food line at the soup kitchen)

Track #4. "AND THOSE DAYS PAID OFF WHEN THE FREMINGER BOLT COMPANY DONATED THE LAST TEN THOUSAND DOLLARS NEEDED TO GET THE TRUCK. THAT WAS LAST MONTH...AND WHO WAS ON THE LINE AT ROGERS TODAY SERVING UP FOOD...FREMINGER'S PRESIDENT BILL FRANNICH."

Bite #4. "We're only happy we can help out. We know how tough it is in these times...and this is our contribution to the county."

(shots of truck pulling away from loading dock and then on the road)

Track #5. "TRUCK DRIVER HENRY WILLIAMS WAS DELIGHTED AS HE MADE HIS LAST DROPOFF ABOUT 5 P.M. AND THEN TOOK THE NEW TRUCK BACK TO THE GARAGE. IT'LL BE IN USE FIVE DAYS EACH WEEK FOR THE NEXT FOUR MONTHS...AND THEN THE FOOD BANK DIRECTORS WILL SEE IF THEY WANT TO RAISE MONEY FOR A SECOND ONE. THIS IS BEN BRILEY REPORTING."

CHAPTER SUMMARY

In the first attempts at the VO, it is hard to get everything right. The concept of a side-by-side narration and video story, each standing on its own, is challenging. Writers must also concentrate on writing and referencing to the timed portion of the spoken text. However, writers must master the process for the VO because it is one of the most popular formats used in local television newscasts in this country.

The VO/SOT is a commonly used television news format. It requires joining a VO story and a soundbite within a tightly compressed framework. It can be expanded to include another VO segment after the bite. Writers composing a VO story should be careful of video placement within the VO portion and the video reference necessary in the writeup.

Television: Packages
and Live Shots

CHAPTER PREVIEW

For years, the field videotape package has been the backbone of television news. Reporters had to plan for these, assemble them, and be familiar with a wide range of package types: the breaking stories, the backgrounders, the features, the *mini-docs.*

Now technology has made life a bit more complex. The ease of setting up live shots, whether on local microwave or by satellite, has complicated the life of the reporter. News managers love to have reporters standing in the street, doing live intros, even hours after events are over. So those getting reporters' jobs now must not only know packages and but also be extremely competent on live shots with a video insert, either tracked or as a VO/SOT/VO.

There is nothing mysterious about either the package or the live shot. Reporters assemble various combinations of interviews, natural sound sequences, *standup bridges* and *closers,* and their own narration tracks into these formats. This chapter highlights the most common ones—hard news, backgrounders, features, and the longer reports, such as a series or mini-docs—and reviews the needs for live shot interior packages.

While both the altered chronology model and the particular-to-general model are useful to reporters in planning packages, the best ones require careful planning and optimum use of video. There is a need to identify good natural sound sequences, and to study various uses of reporter involvement and reporter standups.

GLOSSARY

BRIDGE   A very short (usually under :10) transition used in television news packages. It can be a tracked portion or an on-camera standup.

CLOSER   The reporter's final segment of a package. It might be a track, a standup, or a combination of track and standup.

CUE An agreed-upon action, word, or phrase that is the alert to an upcoming step in whatever production is in progress.

DONUT Slang term for video used in a live shot. This can be either tracked or in the VO/SOT/VO format. Also called an *insert*.

MINI-DOC (for mini-documentary) A longer (2:30–7:00) package that runs during a regular newscast but usually covers a timeless topic or angle and is prepared in advance. The mini-doc may run in segments over the course of several days. Also called a *segment report* or *two-*, *three-*, *four-*, or *five-parter*.

STANDUP The reporter on camera in the field. It could be live but is principally a videotaped segment. Standups are used mostly as bridges and closers.

SHORT PACKAGES

A package is a complete videotaped news story from the field with the reporter's voice tracks narrating the entire segment. They are the meat and potatoes of daily television journalism. Depending on the story complexity, most reporters do one or two packages a day. The shorter packages—anywhere from :45 to 2:00—generally involve breaking news and deadline pressure; the longer features allow time to think and create subtleties with audio and video; the longest—cover stories and mini-doc—are generally more work than you ever thought they'd be.

In these short packages, the video work is subordinate to the journalistic need. Producers and assignment editors, who may or may not have been on the street reporting, regularly demand coverage of stories for which there is no appealing visual element. Reporters often must scramble for visuals to cover assignments on budgets, zoning battles, or education stories, often spending time searching for B-roll (video for illustration) possibilities or using standup bridges and closers to cover nonvisual concepts.

Reporters need to be aware of the power of video and audio to tell a story. In Chapter 10, we discussed the hierarchy of video, from the most effective type of sequences to the least. The top of the line is the NAT SOT sequence without narration, in which the natural audio and the video sequence tells the story.

THE REPORTER-SHOOTER RELATIONSHIP

The combination of a reporter and videographer is the backbone of television news. On any reporting assignment, each has a particular set of jobs that need to be done to make the report viable, and to give it the visual texture that makes it interesting.

Reporters are ultimately responsible for the story. Back at the station, they must choose the visuals and write the narration tracks that will clearly tell the story. When on location, they must direct the shooter to whatever sequences and particular visuals they know they are going to need, as well as staying alert to unusual situations that may need the videographer's attention. They must also respect the shooter's abilities and be cautious not to overstep bounds by overdirecting the artistic content of the shots.

It is the shooter's job, as photojournalist, to report on the visual scenes at the location. Within the reporter's request ("I'll need a sequence of the kids in the playground and a sequence of the parents arriving to pick up the kids"), the shooter must provide a pastiche of shots in the grammar of the sequence—WSs, MSs, CUs, low-angle, high-angle, tracking, tilts, reverses. The videographer is also responsible for the video's technical quality, the lighting of the scene, and the quality of the reporter's appearance on camera as well as what the reporter says in on-camera standups and bridges.

THE STANDARD PARTS OF PACKAGES

A free-lance writer once told me that, after he had submitted an idea to a famous network magazine news program, he met with a producer who liked the proposal. The producer said something like this: "Okay, what's my B-roll, what are my sequences, who are the interviewees, and what kind of access can I get?" The producer was giving the writer a lesson in television news—the litany of the standard parts of packages. You'll be looking for the same kinds of material to combine into your packages.

Visuals and Sequences

This is television. You need pictures to tell the stories, and not just any pictures, but the best available. It almost always means going to a location, to fly in a plane, shoot pictures in a drugstore, attend a grade school class, find a mechanic who's working on a particular type of car, go to a gunshop, or walk a mile with the protestors.

Interviews

Don't waste any time interviewing the wrong persons. Review Chapter 5 on the elements that add value to interviews. Remember, the most effective bites are from eyewitness accounts, someone responding to charges, persons affected by actions in the story, and qualified evaluations.

Standups

The power of standup bridges and closes depends not only on the text but also on the reporter's position in the frame, the background activity, the reporter's movement, and the camera movement.

For the content of standup bridges, look for a way to make a natural transition between points in the story. It could be between two locations, time frames, or subtopics of the story theme. For instance, in a story with two locations, you'll want to do the standup bridge at the beginning of the sequence of the second location. Then decide if you want camera motion (pans or tilts), lens movement (zoom in or zoom back), or reporter activity (walk and talks, arm motions, pointing). For any movement, there must be a reason to draw the camera's focus from one point to the other.

In some cases, you may want to bridge into a soundbite from an interview that is already on tape. That means the last sentence of the bridge must include the writeup. If you do that, also shoot a bridge without the writeup. You may have to dump the interview, and in that case you'll have a backup.

For standup closers, the standard is to talk about the future. For that reason, do the standup in a location related to the story, one that might even have some action in the background.

It is crucial, though, not to think the standups are mandatory parts of breaking news. In short packages, the standups are often outdated or the package structure changed. Don't be afraid to dump useless standups.

Tracks

The narration written for most short packages is severely condensed into a series of tracks. Each track covers a stretch from one sound source to the next one, or from the beginning of the package to the first bite, from soundbite to soundbite, and from the last soundbite to either the story's end or the closing standup. Each track may repeat a few words from the previous soundbite, then include new information and the writeup to the next soundbite. Most novice reporters encounter two problems when writing tracks.

First, they tend to overwrite their packages. They jam too much information into the tracks, stretching out the story and possible upsetting any sense of pacing. Initial tracks should be :30 or less. Interior tracks are often much shorter, and sometimes are only a phrase that bridges between two soundbites.

Second, beginning reporters write tracks about story elements for which there is no video. Covering tracks with wallpaper video might dull the audience interest. If you are short on video, put some information in the studio lead-in or the tag.

THE ORDER FOR PACKAGE DESIGN

1. Evaluate the video.

2. Pull or select the soundbites. Think of the order you'd like them in.

3. Identify the various sequences you have. Choose one to be the first sequence.

4. Evaluate the standups. Should you use the bridge? The closer?

5. Write the lead-in.

6. Write the first track up to the first soundbite.

7. Write the last track or position the standup close.

8. Lay out the bites and write the tracks to bridge them.

9. Evaluate the final plan for time to see if it fits the producer's needs.

This is a typical short package script. It is for a morning package after a fire the previous evening.

Lead-in	FIRE OFFICIALS MAY HAVE AN ANSWER TO WHAT CAUSED CLOSE TO A MILLION DOLLARS DAMAGE TO A DOWNTOWN BUILDING LAST NIGHT.
	ROB BOLIN REPORTS.
Track #1	THE OLD WAREHOUSE ON WALLY STREET HAD BEEN VACANT FOR YEARS. SHORTLY AFTER SEVEN P-M...IT SUDDENLY WENT UP IN FLAMES.
	CAFE OWNER MARIO BIANTIN WATCHED THE BLAZE FROM ACROSS THE STREET.
Bite #1	"One second everything was quiet and the next...there were flames coming out the windows and roof...even before the fire trucks got here."
Track #2	FIREMEN SAY THE BUILDING WAS FULLY INVOLVED WHEN THEY ARRIVED.
	FIRE CAPTAIN ALDEN CARTER SAYS THE WAREHOUSE COULDN'T BE SAVED.
Bite #2	"This type of building has no fire walls and once the thing gets roaring, it's like a locomotive. Nothing can stop it."

Track #3   THE FLAMES COULD BE SEEN
             FOR MILES AND THE SMOKE BLEW
             DIRECTLY ACROSS THE BARNES
             EXPRESSWAY...CHOKING OFF TRAF-
             FIC AT THE END OF THE EVENING
             RUSH HOUR.

             IT TOOK THREE HOURS BEFORE
             THE ROAD WAS OPEN AGAIN.

Standup   (flames are out...shot in morning)
bridge

             AS DAWN BROKE...ARSON INVES-
             TIGATORS PICKED THROUGH THE
             BURNED OUT BUILDING. THEY
             CONCENTRATED THEIR EFFORTS IN
             ONE CORNER BY THE STREET.

Bite #3   "It looks like it started in this area
             where transients sleep. We found
             gasoline and an old camp stove."

Track #4   THE BUILDING'S OWNER SAYS
             THE FIRE MAY HAVE SAVED HIM
             SOME TROUBLE. YESTERDAY...HE
             TOOK OUT A PERMIT TO BEGIN
             THE COSTLY JOB OF TEARING
             DOWN THE PLACE. THAT WAS TO
             HAPPEN NEXT MONTH. THIS IS ROB
             BOLIN FOR K-560 NEWS.

Rules for Package Organization

The two basic narrative models we presented in Chapter 7 can be used and stretched for short package work. The altered chronology model is perfect for a simple report. Some general rules, for all types of reports, are these:

1. *News is about people.* Focus on what people do. Avoid still inanimate objects, empty rooms, wide shots with very little action in them, and overused shots seen again and again until the audience is dulled beyond all reason.

2. *Lead with your best visuals.* Because television news is photojournalism, it is best to evaluate which sequences are best, and try to get these to the first track to attract and hold the viewers. In a recent package about a holiday party at a zoo, a novice reporter opened with shots of people walking into the zoo and a sequence of the zoo signs. Later in the piece, we saw gorillas opening large wrapped Christmas presents and lions tearing into wrapped bales of food. These could have given the reporter a chance for an exciting lead.

3. *Don't use flawed tape, bad audio, or out-of-focus or poorly lit video.* Write the story to include quality video. Simply ignore less-than-perfect images and audio. Don't write them into the package. One reporter recently relied on a spoken interview conducted in a noisy room with the camera mic. Although she knew what the person was saying, it was very hard for a listener to make out what was said.

4. *Let your stories breathe.* Too many reporters jam their stories together, without looking for natural sound to add pauses between tracks and bites, or between parts of tracks. Stories that are wall-to-wall narration are often overbearing and don't make good use of strong visuals. Plan for your reports to "breathe" with a few natural sound seconds here and there.

5. *If stumped for organization, use narrative models.* By now you're a bit weary of hearing the old litany: lead-in, current situation, past or background, controversy or story, and future. This altered chronology model is the backbone of 50 percent of television news stories. You certainly are encouraged to deviate from it, but if it is needed, you can't miss by using it. The same holds true with the particular-to-general model. You can't lose by opening on a person's story.

BEGINNING THE PROCESS

Although there are many assignment types, we'll talk about two. The first is a general topic backgrounder, for which a reporter has to set up shots, interviews, and sequences. The second is a fast-breaking assignment to cover an event with a known interviewee available.

Case 1: The General Topic Assignment

You are given a topic such as the dangers of fatty foods for heart patients. The assignment came off a wire story that morning out of Washington saying there is conclusive evidence that fatty foods increase buildup along artery walls.

In this case, you are free to design the story.

Begin by asking whether there's any part of this story that cannot be told visually, or if told visually, would be dreadful. For this story, you know that on-camera interviews with scientists may be difficult because of the jargon.

Search for a local angle that is a good television story. The national story could be a reader that would set up the lead-in to the local story. Don't forget to find out what local companies, research universities, or hospitals have been doing in the area.

Your first step will be research. Have someone search for the latest information on the fatty food controversy.

Then go through this checklist.

1. Are there possible sequences available, especially ones with NAT SOT that might tell the story?

2. Next, what are the B-roll possibilities? Do we need pictures of fatty foods (as named in the wire story) and can we get those in a grocery store, in a kitchen (commercial or home), or being served to diners? Do we need medical illustration and should we call the local teaching hospital for stills, diagrams, and cross sections of arteries. Would a medical library have computer animation? Do these pictures need to move? Is there file tape of heart operations?

3. For interviews, are there two sides to this controversy? (Are there even more sides?) Do we need spokespeople for both? Can we get help from the American Heart Association, the local teaching hospital, a local cardiologist? What about vox pop? Do we need the general public talking about this?

4. For standups, is there a good location now? Should we be doing a bridge in a research laboratory or at the American Heart Association office?

5. For tracks, am I writing anything I won't be able to cover? For instance, if there is no video of heart surgery, do I want to mention this? Maybe it can go in the standups.

That's how you might plan before you even leave your desk. By this time, you've got some idea of how much trouble it will be to get visuals, how many interviews might be available, and what the day will be like. The other research and the quality of the recorded interviews will give you options about the placement of the bites. You'll probably be able to design this package when you're part of the way through it.

Case 2: The Breaking News Package

Hard news is the daily coverage of crime, government, business, marches, speeches, the courts, confrontations, education, and social activity in expected and unexpected events. In most hard news coverage, reporters and shooters use their previous experiences to gather a competent amount of material on location. At the event, reporters and shooters cover themselves by gathering old comfortable sequence building blocks: lots of WSs, MSs and CUs, cover shots, standup closes and bridges, and interviews. Each knows the structure for the hard news package may come later.

For hard news, the reporter can write the tracks in the truck on the way back to the station. There, the reporter and editor are usually finding visuals to illustrate a report that is narrative driven, meaning the track scripts for short packages are usually written before the pictures are cut; and the visuals are edited to match the flow of the rise and fall of the reporter's voice.

For short packages, the crew may have limited opportunities for pictures: possibly only one or two locations and repetitive sequences. So work hard on location to shoot as much as you can. Before you get back in the car, know how much of the story refers to pictures of kids at a child care center and how much time it'll take to get enough B-roll to tell the story. Know if there will be NAT SOUND sequences? Can these be useful in telling the story? Will you need two different sequences from the same location and can that be shot?

Do you need illustrations? Do you need file tape? Do you need one, two, three, or many interviews?

Writing a Package Script

Write a :10 lead-in and a 1:20 package for the following situation. You have three bites and you will need four tracks. You can use the bites in any order you wish. You may also invent sequences you will need and would like to have. Write these invented sequences in parentheses at the beginning of each track.

Situation

You have three soundbites on a story about the supervisors getting ready to vote on a new downtown height limit for buildings in one neighborhood—the Rose District. This is coming up for a vote tonight, but everyone thinks it will pass.

The new plan will allow 24-story buildings in the Rose District, which is an older part of town adjacent to the new high-rise buildings in the Center District. Currently the Rose has a two-story height limit.

The new plan will allow high-rise buildings in the area, which is now a hodgepodge of older bungalow-style homes. Needless to say, all of the labor unions and construction-related businesses are for the plan. Most of the supervisors also appear to like the idea. Neighborhood residents have been fighting the plan, but this is a working class district and they don't have much clout with city hall. They haven't been able to raise enough money to really fight it.

Supervisor Rod Stern TRT :08
"We must move ahead with building in this city. No district can tie our hands because they don't want development there."

Architect Anna Chavez-Rinaldo TRT :13
"It doesn't mean there will be a flood of skyscrapers built there. There are plenty of limits on the bulk of buildings anywhere in town."

Long-time resident Maria Ramirez TRT :10
"Sure, the supervisors are going to go ahead and hand over our district to the developers. They all live in Mar Vista Estates, which you can bet will stay two stories."

LIVE SHOTS

Portable microwave equipment first became popular in the mid-1970s, but was usually limited to larger markets which could afford the quarter-million-dollar costs of the live trucks. Now the technology is cheaper and there are more options for routing signals. Constant live coverage has been so successful that people expect it in every story. Probably the most ironic live coverage came in Somalia, when US Navy seals, staging a night landing on a Somalian beach, found themselves arriving to face television lights, reporters, and live coverage to American television screens. In the 1990s, medium-market and even small-market stations bought live vans, satellite uplink trucks, and repeater dishes, and they've been sending local crews to international stories, piggybacking on network satellite uplinks. There is no doubt now that live reporting has changed local broadcast news practices forever.

Local reporters need to have thick skins about live shots. News managers and station chiefs want as many live inserts as possible, even on stories long since over. Reporters have to be competent in doing live intros and field tags. A journalist who cannot speak extemporaneously on camera should think twice about continuing in this profession.

There are ethical problems as well. Anyone in broadcast journalism is aware that people in the community begin events to coincide with live newscasts, playing to the known need for live shots during the program. Because everyone is aware of this, it is important for reporters and producers to consider to what extent they are being used.

Producers must be cautious about hype and overuse of the "live" possibility for stories. Although live shots can be wonderfully effective as a means of expanding the studio, care should be taken that the technology is not used merely as a means of advertising the news staff.

When faced with a live shot, assignment editors and producers must always ask if there are more effective and economical ways of telling the story. Will there be better clarity and presentation from the studio? Sometimes, they may have to argue against station policies for extensive live coverage.

News staffs need to watch that their editorial values are not compromised by the live shot. Because so much of the report comes from a live standup in the field, editorial control of a story's details is minimal and, although there are cellular phones and portable fax machines for scripts, errors can creep into the story. Watch carefully that the production demands for a live location presence don't eliminate the care a staff might give to a story back in the newsroom.

Live Shot Possibilities

Once the crew establishes a clear signal to the station, the location live shot can take many forms. It can be anything from a field-based mini-newscast to a fairly routine studio toss to live shot, video insert, live tag, and back to the studio. Many times, it is so smoothly done that the audience isn't aware of the planning and technology needed to produce it. The live shot format has many possibilities.

- a standup with no video
- a standup with the reporter doing a VO
- a standup with the reporter doing a VO/SOT/VO
- a standup wrapped around a package (called a *donut*)
- a "Q-&-A" or "debrief" with the reporter
- a live interview by the reporter
- a reporter split screen with another reporter
- a reporter working as part of a round robin, and tossing to another reporter
- a standup with video fed from the field
- a standup using video pre-fed and edited at the station

The format combinations are fascinating and a little bit dangerous. It is crucial that writers and producers communicate with reporters about what material is available. Are the VO pictures usable? Did everything come in all right? Do we have a roll cue? Is the anchor going to ask a question? Will it be a question for which the reporter knows the answer?

Writing strategies are as endless as the format combinations. In some ways, live shots give the reporters quite a bit of latitude in story assembly. Everything is less rigid, and except for the video work in the donut insert, the structure can be informal.

Script format varies from station to station; however, most examples have the normal lead-in, notes about the field intro script and then the all-important cues to the time to roll, insert sound and CGs, and return to live and return to studio.

Some Important Rules in Live Shot Design

1. The toss to the reporter should not steal the reporter's story. The reporter should write the toss and flow smoothly into the field open.

2. The field open should always set the stage if the toss didn't. Saying something like "IT'S QUIET RIGHT NOW BUT JUST THREE HOURS AGO..." helps explain why a reporter is standing at night in an empty field when everyone else has gone home.

3. Get to the video donut as soon as possible. It can be set up as a VO into a tracked package and then come out as a VO at the end, or it can be set up with a natural sound buffer at the top and then be a completely tracked package without a standup.

4. The field tag or closer should report the future and be ready for a Q-&-A if that is set up.

A sample live shot script might look like this.

SPEED LAB/jnh

_____O/C POLICE IN DOWNY FALLS HAVE BROKEN UP WHAT IS BEING CALLED THE LARGEST DRUG LAB EVER FOUND IN CLAY COUNTY.

AUTHORITIES HAVE ARRESTED 12-SUSPECTS AND SEIZED OVER ONE MILLION DOLLARS WORTH OF LAB EQUIPMENT.

REPORTER MARCUS BROWN IS STANDING BY LIVE.

MARCUS?

REMOTE ON CAM (rem)

POLICE HERE TONIGHT AREN'T SAYING HOW THEY FOUND THE LAB...ONLY THAT IT WAS A LONG INVESTIGATION.

VO (vo)

(Pics of police carrying boxes from suburban house)

ALL DAY LONG...THE CRIME LAB HAS BEEN LOADING UP EVIDENCE AND TAKING SAMPLES FROM THIS HOUSE IN THE ROSE DISTRICT.

A POLICE SPOKESMAN SAID IT TOOK THEM A LONG TIME TO BUST THIS OPERATION.

SOT (begins) (sot—police captain Elroy Hirsch)

"We've been after them for two years but we really hit the jackpot here."

Track #1

(Pics of evidence spread out on a table)

> AND QUITE A JACKPOT IT WAS.
> OVER ONE MILLION DOLLARS WORTH
> OF EQUIPMENT AND FINISHED DRUGS
> WORTH OVER TWO MILLION
> DOLLARS ON THE STREET.
> POLICE SAY THE CASE IS PRETTY
> GOOD AGAINST THE SUSPECTS.

SOT (continues)

> (sot—district attorney Wade Willson)
> "We have twelve suspects and all are
> being charged with felonies. I think
> we've got the central core of this
> operation."

VO   (vo)

(Pics of suspects walking out of courtroom)

> NOW THE ARRAIGNMENT FOR ALL
> SUSPECTS IS SET FOR NEXT TUESDAY.

REMOTE ON CAM   (rem on cam)

> POLICE STILL AREN'T SAYING IF
> THERE WILL BE MORE ARRESTS.
> THAT'S ALL FROM HERE TONIGHT...
> THIS IS MARCUS BROWN REPORTING
> FROM THE ROSE DISTRICT.

Live Shot Exercise

You need to turn out a live-shot script to cover this situation. You are standing at 10 p.m. in the empty parking lot outside the civic auditorium in the suburbs of Steeltown.

Situation

Noted television producer of violent programs Cruella Barnes has now come out against all the gunplay and murders on the tube. She is staging a nationwide speaking tour, claiming that all of her scripts will now feature endings that involve what is called "conflict resolution," a means of defusing tensions. She is speaking tonight at a local civic auditorium and has a wildly enthusiastic audience applauding everything she says. For visuals you have a number of scenes from her earlier violent programs, some file tape of a network executive testifying before a congressional committee about violence, some NAT SOT of her speech tonight, and some shots of people watching television at a local electronics sales store.

CRUELLA SOT :10
"I just hope it isn't too late to reverse the damage that I have done."

NETWORK EXEC Adrianne Lister :15
"Miss Barnes' conversion comes at an odd time, just when her string of endless trashy programs were losing audience appeal. We are waiting to see how genuine it is."

PSYCHOLOGIST Herman Goertz :12
"It's been clear for a long time that children are deeply affected by violence on television."

LONGER PACKAGES

Longer packages might run anywhere from 2:00 to 7:00. Generally they cover timeless topics from hard news backgrounders to special profiles, investigative reports, mini-docs, or sidebars. The longest ones have special names, such as segment reports, cover stories, three-part team reports, and so on. In contrast to the short-term general-assignment daily reporting, the planning, construction, editing, and writing of longer reports are quite different.

Research for Longer Packages

Research can be carried out for days and sometimes weeks. Interviews can be used for research. More detailed data can be pursued. Quite often the original planning for B-roll and sequences changes many times. A potential drawback of longer packages is the lack of an angle to the story. Research may be too global. Too wide a theme makes it hard to maintain interest.

Shooting for Longer Packages

On long packages, more preparation is possible and the same crew should work on all assignments. B-roll is more comprehensive. The influence of lucky shots, often exploited in shorter packages, is not even considered. Aesthetic values in shooting are higher and more relationship shots are expected.

A problem with multiday shooting schedules is that the story may change. Week-old interviews may become dated. As the story evolves, new sequences are added and old ones, even these that are the result of hours of shooting, are discarded.

Interviewing for Longer Packages

Interviewing is more relaxed and informal and requires less immediate goal-oriented answers. Reporters are usually better prepared and can proceed in a more dialogue-like format. Better and longer cutaways on all interviews are possible. Parts of interviews can be used for research. Because there is less structure, there will be more waste in interviews for longer packages. Sometimes, because production values are higher, entire interviews will be discarded.

All interviews should be transcribed. This gives reporters or producers a better chance to craft silky writeups. It is also easier to use longer sound bites.

Writing for Longer Packages

The quality of writing should be much higher and more fluid than for short packages. It is possible to write and rewrite tracks to support polished and edited sequences. Writers and editors can preview rough cuts and re-edit as needed.

A common problem with longer pieces is that broadcast workers have trouble completing a story. Producers or reporters do too much gathering and too little planning and so can become overwhelmed by the material.

Reporter Standups

Standups are written after everything else is shot and finished. They should add information. Their placement is more often used to vary the visual elements of the story while establishing relationships between angles and elements within the story.

Production Values

Production quality should be much higher in long packages. Better visuals, longer time to edit, little need to stay within restrictive formats are all benefits for the long package producer.

Note, however, that postproduction time is much longer. A 2:30 piece for daily news might take one hour to edit. A 3:00 piece that is looked at as a longer package might take five hours to edit. A 5:00 package might take all day to edit, as well as to insert special visuals, music, and documentary effects in it.

CHAPTER SUMMARY

Television packages come in different lengths with different rules for composing scripts. In short packages, up to 2:30 in length, the reporter or producer is often forced to find visuals to cover a journalistic need. These are generally categorized into breaking stories under heavy deadline pressure and more generic theme stories in which the reporter may have more flexibility in finding visuals.

The popularity of live shots has forced most reporters to learn the various combinations involved in remote work. The writing in the live shot can be more informal than in other formats.

In longer packages, the reporter or producer generally sets the story theme around easily obtainable and visually appealing segments. In each of these formats, it is important to consider the sequences, interviews, standup possibilities, and production values.

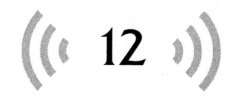

12

Producing for All Media: Developing Stories

CHAPTER PREVIEW

In previous chapters we've covered the work of the newswriter or reporter. Now, this next-to-last chapter begins with the duties of the producer. The producer is the gatekeeper, the editor, the story developer, the resources coordinator, the copyeditor, the legal backstop—in general, the one responsible for the quality and production of the newscast. The producer may assign stories to writers, select the angle and story length, and then coach the writer through difficult stages of the story before examining the script for accuracy, fairness, comprehensive coverage, perspective, opinion, libel, invasion of privacy, and adherence to station writing style. The finished story is then ready for inclusion in the newscast. Chapter 13 will examine how the newscasts should be structured.

GLOSSARY

ADVANCING THE STORY   A producer's job, seeing that the story isn't stale and filled with old news. New sources must be contacted and updates made a part of the story.

GATEKEEPING   The process of choosing, developing, editing, and eventually sequencing stories for the newscast. Gatekeeping also involves eliminating stories.

STRINGER   An independent reporter or shooter who covers stories with hopes of selling the results to a station.

THE PRODUCER AS GATEKEEPER

The initial role of the producer is to decide which stories are destined for the newscast and then to see that these stories are developed in the time before the newscast. To do this, a producer has to be abreast of current events, following local, national, and international stories. A producer should be informed on continuing stories and be able to think beyond the simple stories that are prominent that day. A producer should have a sense for covering upcoming events. A producer should be willing to take chances, even run outside the format box occasionally to cement a solid journalistic story. A producer should promote enterprise on the part of reporters and staff members, constantly urging them to check and recheck stories, find new sources, get new reactions, and always advance the story.

THE PRODUCER'S JOB

Long before the producer coaches the writer or copyedits the story, the producer's stamp goes on the newscast. The formation of stories begins during the assignment stage, where the producer's needs often lead to different angles or visual coverage. After that, the producer's job is to evaluate the stories for content and length, stack the stories into a newscast, coach and copyedit, and make certain that everything gets finished and on the air. There are five principal tasks: (1) finding and evaluating stories, (2) developing and assigning stories, (3) coaching and copyediting, (4) stacking the newscast, and (5) making on-air decisions. We will cover (4) and (5) in the next chapter.

The News of the Day

Producers should listen to, watch, and read all major news sources as the day develops, even before they get to the office. Sometimes it is necessary to call the newsroom to see that the major stories are being covered, expanded, and updated.

At the office, most good producers maintain a list of must-run stories and minor stories that will be possibilities for the newscast. One way to do it is to use a simple diagram called a roughsheet (see Figure 12.1).

Must-run video stories	Must-run readers
Minor video stories	Minor readers

FIGURE 12.1
Example of a producer's working roughsheet.

The producer carries the story list everywhere, adding to it and crossing off stories that don't pan out. Stories in the must-run video side or even the must-run readers should be constantly developed by looking for outside help in visuals, tape trades, satellite services and network feeds, stringer footage, wire stories, and so on. If you have newswriters, be sure they can access the latest information on workstation screens. Other tips on producing the day's newscast follow:

- Check and prepare the HFR (hold for release) stories you have ready. Make sure the lead-ins are written into script form, the CGs are ordered, and timing is checked on the tapes. These stories can be blocked into your newscast.

- Once you have a lead story in mind, go all out on the coverage of this one. Make certain that there aren't any holes in the journalistic and mechanical coverage of it. Perhaps you need to assign a writer early in the day to tie together all the loose ends of the story.

- Maintain the running list of the minor stories and check this throughout the day to see if you've missed anything. Begin to pass out writing assignments on the more important stories.

- Don't kill any stories until you get near the newscast. It's always better to work with options; however, don't commit writers to marginal stories until you know you'll need those stories.

- Don't vacillate. Make decisions and then follow up on them. Say yes or no. Take control of the newscast.

Developing Stories

The way to develop stories is to advance the information and to look for extra visuals or sidebar stories, interviews, and reports to fill in the gaps. Advancing the story is accomplished by updating all of the information and double-checking sources. As an example, coverage can be expanded if the producer takes these steps to develop a simple :25 wire story on a forest fire:

1. Contact someone to get visuals of the fire. This will provide more information to viewers.

2. Get computer artists to make a map of the area.

3. Have the assignment desk send a reporter to the scene. Set up a live report. It will work with VO and map.

4. Have a researcher check out past fires in the area. Pull file tape if necessary.

5. Have a reporter feed VO/SOT insert for a live shot.

6. Check to see whether any HFRs on fire danger are available. By the end of this step, you'll have a studio lead-in with a map, a live shot with a VO/SOT insert, and a backgrounder to follow all that. You'll have easily 6:00 of material. You might have to cut it down.

7. See if the graphic artists can come up with an OTS (over-the-shoulder) topic box for the story. See if there is one already in the still store that is usable.

Assigning Stories

When certain that some stories will be in the newscast, the producer can assign them a story time TST, a format (READER/ VO/ VO/SOT/ LIVE SHOT), and decide what visuals, such as OTS topic boxes and full-screen visuals, should be included.

At that point, the producer should assign the stories to other producers, newswriters, or anchors to write. At smaller stations, the producer will probably write some of the stories too.

Reviewing Scripts

Once the writer has finished, the story is ready for copyediting, a process that demands great attention to detail. The producer or news editor should examine the story, looking for errors of fact, of law, and of style. If any of these holes in the story are found, the story should be returned to the writer.

Accuracy. Accuracy is the first and the most important consideration in the editing of any story. A story must be as accurate as possible relative to the information known at that time. There can be no compromise in this area. Copyeditors can check for accuracy by:

- *Reviewing sources.* Any doubts about the quality of primary or secondary sources must be conveyed to the audience. Double check source copy.

- *Questioning jargon.* Is any backgrounding needed?

- *Reviewing adjectives* for sensationalism or loose story assumptions.

Producers, if they are separate from copyeditors, must also check all actualities (radio) or visuals (television):

- *Checking all video packages.* Producers should review the scripts and look at the package when possible. There should be no surprises in the newscast.

- *Checking the referencing of every actuality or soundbite.* Those with no writeup and cold intros must be reviewed.

- *Checking visuals.* All OTS topic boxes must be checked for intent, and any full-screen CGs must be checked to see if the graphic artist carried out the intent of the newswriter.

Checking Source Copy

Review the wire copy to see if the broadcast script which follows conforms to it. In this case, the producer assigned a :30 reader.

PARIS, France (RPG)...The health benefits of red wine are in the news again and this time the news is good, according to the French.

At this year's Vinexpo, the world's largest wine exposition held here every two years, scientists and doctors did their best to leave the impression that moderate wine consumption of red wine is great for the health.

The reason for the optimism is a new series of studies that show that the tannins in red wine increase the amount of free oxygen in the blood and prevent cholesterol pockets from forming, producing an effect similar to aspirin, said Rene Parquet, chief officer of the French wine exporting group Vin Monde.

French officials pointed out that this comes only from red wine and not white, not an unusual claim to be made in this city of Bordeaux, known the world over for its rich red wines.

European grape growers are concerned about new anti-alcohol laws that are popping up in Europe and around the globe. "There has been an increase in alcohol related legislation and it's not been the best for us," said Jacques Jerboa, a leading exporter. "Governments think they can solve their addiction problems by legislating against wine when drugs and cheap alcohol drinks are the problems," he added.

Examples of the laws are prohibitions on advertising and sales of alcohol drinks on television and in certain periodicals in countries such as the United States. "These must be carefully reviewed," said one French official.

U.S. importer Vins de France of New Jersey president Robert Vintage said it's unlikely that the new French research will change any laws. "We must learn to get the word out in any way we can, and we'll continue to do this. It's clear the public is happy keeping alcohol advertising off TV, thinking this will stop their kids from drinking," Vintage added.

(continued)

WINE/jnh

_____O/C   NEW RESEARCH IS SAYING IT'S OKAY TO
HAVE A GLASS OF WINE WITH MEALS...AND
THAT THIS IS REALLY A HEALTH BENEFIT.

    THE STUDIES COME FROM FRANCE...AND
CAME TO LIGHT DURING THE WORLD'S
LARGEST INTERNATIONAL WINE EXPOSITION
IN BORDEAUX. RESEARCHERS SAY A SINGLE
GLASS OF WINE WILL HELP RELEASE OXYGEN
IN THE BLOOD.

    THAT OXYGEN IS A BIG HELP IN REMOVING
SOME OF THE CHOLESTEROL THAT HAS BUILT
UP IN ARTERIES.

    THE FRENCH SAY IT'S HARD TO GET THE
WORD OUT THOUGH.

    FRENCH WINE EXECUTIVE ROBERT VINTAGE
SAYS THERE ARE TOO MANY LAWS AGAINST
WINE ADVERTISING AND THAT SOMETHING
SHOULD BE DONE ABOUT IT.

Accuracy

Examine this story for accuracy. Even without the source material, an editor should suspect some areas. Circle any possible problem material.

_____O/C   DIVORCE IS BECOMING THE FINAL STAGE IN THE MAJORITY OF MARRIAGES IN CLAY COUNTY.

RECORDS AT THE CLERK'S OFFICES SHOW THERE HAVE BEEN 15 MORE DIVORCES THAN WEDDINGS IN THE PAST 12 MONTHS.

COUNTY CLERK MALOU CRUZ SAYS SHE THINKS IT'S A BREAKDOWN OF FAMILY VALUES IN THE YOUNGER GENERATION.

CRUZ SAID PEOPLE JUST DON'T TRY TO STICK IT OUT THROUGH HARD TIMES ANYMORE LIKE THEY USED TO.

ONE LOCAL MINISTER CALLED THE TREND ALARMING. THE REVEREND AMOS WILLIAMS SAYS HE HAS HEARD THE DIVORCE RATE IS 75-PERCENT IN THE COUNTY.

Fairness Although we can understand how reporters may become sympathetic to one side in a story, most news organizations attempt to represent fairly the position of any side in a dispute. Fairness can be difficult to achieve at times because news reporters don't have the luxury of time to contact everyone involved in the stories. Scripts should be checked to see whether writers have made an effort to obtain all sides of the story, and to clearly portray these without bias. By being fair, you show your audience that you believe they have the brains to form their own conclusions.

(((**EXERCISE 12-C**)))

Fairness

Examine this story for fairness. Circle any areas to check.

_____ O/C   A CITIZEN'S ENVIRONMENTAL COMMITTEE IS
ACCUSING A RICHMOND AREA REFINERY OF
KNOWINGLY LEAKING MILLIONS OF GALLONS
OF DIESEL FUEL INTO THE CARAHOMA RIVER.
THE GROUP...CALLING ITSELF CITIZENS
AGAINST POLLUTION...OR CAP...BLAMES THE
GASTRON REFINERY FOR TEN CHEMICAL SPILLS
IN THE PAST 15-MONTHS.
A CAP SPOKESWOMAN SAID THE REFINERY
DID THIS SECRETLY AT NIGHT AND FAILED TO
NOTIFY THE POLLUTION CONTROL DISTRICT.
WE WERE UNABLE TO CONTACT THE
REFINERY FOR A RESPONSE.

Comprehensive Coverage   Well-researched stories should be able to answer all questions about the story. For each story, try answering these questions.

1. Have all the angles been covered?

2. Do we know enough about the background of people or groups involved in this story to make judgments?

((• EXERCISE 12-D •))

Scope

Examine this story for scope. Circle any words that represent areas about which you need more information.

_____O/C   THE BANK OF ST. MILLS IS ANNOUNCING IT WILL FILE A LAWSUIT AGAINST A FORMER EMPLOYEE TO RECOVER MILLIONS OF DOLLARS IN BAD LOANS.

A BANK'S OFFICER...BOB SHIELDS...HAD APPROVED ALL THE LOANS...SECURING THE DEALS WITH LOCAL PROPERTY. THE BANK IS CHARGING THAT SHIELDS PROFITED ON EACH DEAL.

THE LOANS ARE NOT IN DEFAULT...BUT ARE QUESTIONABLE AND BANK SOURCES SAID THE LOSSES COULD GO AS HIGH AS 23-MILLION DOLLARS.

BANK OFFICIALS SAY SHIELDS IS ON VACATION IN SOUTH AMERICA.

Other Checks   Producers must examine all the stories for problems with libel, slander, and invasion of privacy (see Chapter 2) and also review them for use of the station's writing style (see Chapter 3). Producers must also review the stories for plausibility and reliance on questionable sources. If the stories need adjustment, it is best to return them to the writer with a note on what must be done.

Coaching Writers

The producer's continuing job while the story is in progress is to coach the writer to produce a better story. Roy Peter Clark and Don Fry explain this process in detail in their helpful book *Coaching Writers: Editors and Reporters Working Together* (New York: St. Martin's Press, 1992). According to Clark and Fry, this coaching is a method of assisting reporters who might have hit a block while preparing the story. The coaching takes little time, and is a matter of listening and asking questions to stimulate the writer's creative process. The intention is to help the writer identify the key problems with the story, ask questions that will help the writer plan his or her own revisions, and motivate the writer to make those changes. All this is done, the authors point out, without the producer being openly critical, taking over the story, or making changes.

This type of coaching helps in two ways: it develops the staff's talents and allows the producer to think about other items without having to rewrite every lead.

CHAPTER SUMMARY

The producer's job begins with a survey of all possible stories for the newscast. From this list, stories will be chosen to be developed, assigned, and then copyedited. Each story is checked for accuracy, fairness, scope of coverage, legal problems, and writing style.

13

Creating Effective Newscasts

CHAPTER PREVIEW

The producer's job is to build an effective newscast, whether it is for broadcast radio, the Internet, or television. Certain concerns go into the format, or *stacking*, as it is called. Producers must understand effective presentation, the endurance of an audience, and limits and qualities of both stories and reporters. Stacking the newscast must be done with an eye to production limits of the different media.

GLOSSARY

BACKTIME   The start time for a newscast story, if the newscast is to end at the scheduled time. This process is usually handled by computer formats; however, in smaller stations it is still done by hand. The backtime is most efficient when expressed in real clock time, rather than the elapsed time of the newscast.

CLUSTERING   Sequencing stories of a similar theme or topic in newscasts.

NEWS HOLE   The time devoted to news stories in a newscast.

STACKING THE NEWSCAST   The procedure for ordering stories within the timed segments of the newscast. Also known as *formatting*. Normally, the producer or editor stacks the newscast, but at smaller stations, the newscaster may do this.

TEASE   A short item that is designed to attract listeners or viewers to a late story in the newscast. In television, video may be used with the tease.

TOSS   A short item designed to make the transition from one newscaster to the other.

GENERAL CONSIDERATIONS FOR NEWSCAST PRODUCERS

Important Stories First

Newspapers have always put the most important stories on the front page. This provides the readers with cues about story importance. Research has shown that the audience gives more emphasis to stories on the front page or in the lead positions in newscasts. The listeners and viewers assume that if you think it's important, you'll put it first.

For broadcast, the position within the newscast is important. You should have major breaking stories at the top of the newscast. This is the place to find the top stories, crime stories, and harder stories with more tragedy.

In commercial newscasts with segments, though, some of the rules change. At commercial stations, because of the 2:00 ad breaks, you have several segments in a newscast. So instead of one long timeline, you have a series of smaller segments; this means a hard news story can be a B segment lead, and therefore be farther down in the newscast.

Backgrounders in the Middle

Producers attempt to fill the middle of the newscast with longer and more involved stories that explain conditions or change within the community. Usually these are not timely stories, but are major investigations, profiles or obits, enterprise features or hard science, education or community issue stories.

Upbeat and Feature Stories Later

The last third of a newscast is generally a good spot to run cultural stories and advancers for community events. It is a place to wind down and, for that reason, hard tragic stories are kept from the back half of the newscast.

It is a broadcast cliché that warm, upbeat features are found in the last third of the newscast. If the producer finds a kicker, or lighter story, it will go last. Critics have charged that news producers go looking for these types of stories, and exclude real news in order to fit a highly stylized story into a preordained newscast formula. In a way, they're probably right, but still it seems to be a workable formula.

As long as you remain flexible, using features and kickers is not a flawed plan, nor a bad use of the constrained time frame your newscasts have. There are many types of news stories each day, and selections should come from a variety of categories. Anyone who offers the public repetitive sameness of a single category of news is also guilty of finding stories to fit a mold. On heavy news days, you can vary the proportion of major stories to features. On light news days, the proportion floats the other way.

Clustering

There are many theories about what makes a good newscast. It has been proposed that stories of a similar nature or themes should be presented together, or *clustered,* to help the audience focus on the issues and allow a producer easy segues.

On the other hand, some broadcasters believe this is dangerous. They argue that minor stories derive too much importance from being joined to major stories, even if the theme or topic is similar. Opponents of clustering argue that an audience that gets too much of one topic at one time will tune out. Five crime stories in a row, four fire stories, or three back-to-back recreation stories will not serve your purposes.

An acceptable compromise might be to look for short clusters, but stack them cautiously, and include them in the newscast only when the stories are of equal weight and topic. Limit the clusters to two stories.

Headlining Stories That Come Later

Often, continuing national stories become tedious over a period of weeks. The entire country was tired of the Florida recount stories that ran for over a month in the 2000 election. Knowing that these stories are important, but not wanting to dedicate the entire first half of the newscast to this one story day after day, producers took to offering headlines on the Florida story at the top of the newscast and then teasing to an expanded story later in the newscast. It was a good compromise, allowing the story to be covered, while allowing a long-suffering audience to hear other news.

Wraps

In producing, wraps are two or three similar-topic stories that you will have written into one all-inclusive story. This is different from a cluster. While clusters simply put stories with similar themes in adjacent positions, wraps combine two or three stories under a common lead into a single tightly formatted story.

For instance, a wrap may bring together three minor fire stories, all with VOs, resulting in a newsreel look. The new story would get a slug of Wrap/Fire, have a TST of :50, and include three separate items. Wraps are handy formats, but can seem overdone if too many appear in one newscast.

Segues

You should always be on the lookout for possible segues. Go from an international story on exports to a local business story. Go from a statewide story on school funding to local school decisions. The stories are not exactly clustered but are still tied in some way or other. These segues can give you a smooth transition between anchors.

NEWSCAST FORMATS DIFFER

Commercial Versus Noncommercial

Producers who work at noncommercial news stations generally have a single running newscast without any breaks. This simplifies the stacking of stories, but also gives the producer no breaks for correcting misfortunes if anything happens while the newscast is on the air. Commercial breaks are great pauses in the newscast to regroup if a feed machine breaks down or a live remote report bombs out.

Producers who work at commercial stations must be aware of the breaks in the newscast. Each break produces a new segment and each segment will have its own rationale for story flow. Generally the segments are designated by letters A, B, C, and so on, and the individual stories by numbers. Eventually, a story may carry the number B-1 or C-12, and that is how all production staff members will refer to it.

Single Versus Multiple Anchors

A single-anchor newscast is easy. All graphics face a certain way and no tosses have to be written. Other than pacing the stories, little design goes into completing the rundown or stack of the newscast.

A double-anchor newscast provides the producer with a myriad of questions. How often should we make the change from one anchor to the other? Will it be a toss or split story to make the shift? Will we shift coming out of a story, or a package, or should both anchors be on camera at any particular time? If so, are the cameras available and not being used for side anchors? Most of these decisions are built into the format, but each requires an extra amount of plotting and design.

Pacing

Producers, anchors, and news directors forever argue about the pacing—the flow of the newscast. On days when you have three major consensus stories, all with active videotape, live shots, Q-&-A interviews, and sidebars, the producer will be a hero.

But on no-news days, when there is not even agreement on a possible lead story, the producer has to work to keep up the pace. Put three short packages in a row and the top of the newscast may zing along, but you'll have run out of good material and the back half will be slow. Stack three very important but nonvisual reader stories in a row, even if there's nothing visual of the same caliber that could take their place, and you will be criticized for slowing down the pacing. Producers die a thousand deaths on the bad news days.

Predictability

There are different theories about how predictable a newscast should be. Some producers set up segments exactly the same way every day. First segment, 8:00 long, opens with anchor A reading a breaking local story (doesn't have to be a major one), switches to B for one national story, switches back to A for local story with videotape package, switches to B for two local VOs, switches back to A for another local package (upbeat), and then B does the tease across break and before commercial. Second segment starts on A with wrap of three national stories, then to B, and so on.

While it's nice to have a format, it's bad to get locked into it. Sometimes there is no good local story and you should lead with a national or international item. Sometimes, the first eight stories should be national. Argue for flexibility.

Avoid Predictable Pingponging

On newscasts with a double-anchor format, producers often switch anchors on almost every story to keep up the pacing. This is known as *pingponging,* and too much of it becomes very disconcerting to watch. A solution is to vary the number of stories each anchor reads, avoid predictable changes, and when the anchor reads a second or even a third story in a row, to turn the anchor to another camera.

Teases

Part of a producer's job is to write the teases. These are formatted story positions before the newscast or before commercial breaks within the newscast. The well-written tease is a valuable tool for smoothing the continuity. Research has shown it is beneficial to present an audience with an agenda, and teases accomplish this.

The essence of good tease writing is to offer highlights of the story without giving away the details or the results of any actions. A tease with too many details would sound like this:

THE AIRCRAFT CARRIER SEAGULL IS HOME AGAIN AFTER A SIX-MONTH TOUR IN THE MIDDLE EAST. THAT STORY IS COMING UP.

A better tease would allude to the story and tap into keywords that might interest many. Try this one:

A JOYFUL HOMECOMING FOR MANY NAVY FAMILIES. THAT STORY IS COMING UP.

Great care must be used to avoid bamboozling your audience with a sensationalized tease. Viewers and listeners can be offended if the tease doesn't live up to its hype.

ALL OF DOWNTOWN IS DESTROYED BY FIRE. THAT STORY IS COMING UP NEXT.

Viewers wait for the story only to find that it is a downtown in a remote Peruvian village. They feel cheated and rightly so.

Great care must also be used to avoid giving away the payoff in the tease. Leave it up in the air. For instance,

THE ZONING BOARD VOTES TO APPROVE THE NEW MALL NIGHTCLUB. THAT STORY IS NEXT.

In this tease, you've told them the story. They don't have to stick around for it. Instead, try this:

THE ZONING BOARD MAKES A CONTROVERSIAL DECISION ON THE MALL NIGHTCLUB. THAT STORY IS NEXT.

((· EXERCISE 13-A ·))

Writing Teases

Study the situations. Prepare a short tease for each situation to alert viewers that the story is coming up later in the newscast. Work on a separate sheet.

Situation 1

A local citizens' crime study committee has suggested a review of the management policies of the chief of police.

Situation 2

Thieves vandalized a local church just two days before a big holiday that celebrated the Church community's ethnic history.

Situation 3

A well-known and local semiprofessional baseball team needs one more league win to make it to the league finals in Los Angeles.

Situation 4

Former members of a cult are taking their guru to court, claiming he imprisoned them and wouldn't let them leave the group's mountain retreat.

Situation 5

Air Force One, with the president on board, comes within a half mile of colliding with a small private plane near the Denver Airport.

Tosses

One of the producer's jobs is to make seamless tosses between newscasters on the set and in the field. Usually, there is a format for this, but often the tosses have to be composed under extreme deadline pressure. Here are some suggestions.

1. *Ad lib toss.* This is really no toss at all. It is dangerous because newscasters often have lots to think about and don't have the time to come up with a clever ad lib. If you assign an ad lib toss, be prepared for disaster.

2. *Name toss.* This is when someone turns and says the name of the reporter or newscaster without mentioning the story. It can be useful but when repeated again and again, it is dreary.

3. *Toss to personality with generic topic.* This often signals that the producer has run out of ideas for a toss. "Now here's reporter Lucy Watkins with a story on cattle." It's not very exciting.

4. *Toss to the story.* This is one of the two viable methods of segueing from one anchor to a reporter. It's a good idea to always toss to the story and then include the reporter's name.

  IT'S NOT OFTEN WE SEE ELEPHANTS ON THE STREETS OF STEEL-TOWN. REPORTER LARRY DOVBRUSH HAS THAT STORY. LARRY?

5. *Split-story toss.* Both anchors appear in a two-shot. The first anchor reads the headline or top half of the story. The second anchor picks up the story and turns to a camera and completes it on a single-anchor shot. This is an easy and very effective shift. News managers like it because it puts both anchors on at the same time and shows they are working together.

Junk Pages

Teases, tosses, hellos, opens, and goodbyes are often called the *junk pages,* because they are the parts of the station's news format that retain the same basic makeup day after day. Producers simply fill in the blanks with a new story each day.

STACKING THE NEWSCAST

Stacking is the process of filling in the story rundown by deciding on the story content and length, story order, and the pacing of visuals. You'll also have to figure in commercial spots, teases, and tosses. Here are some thoughts about stacking newscasts.

Step One—Figure the News Hole

The first step in producing is to find out how much news you will need for the newscast that day. Finding the actual length of the news hole is a simple process.

Take the station log for the newscast and subtract the time the newscast goes on the air from the time it goes off and you will have the length of the newscast. From that number, subtract any commercials, the junk pages of teases, hellos and goodbyes, theme music, credits, and regularly produced features such as sports and weather. What you are left with is called the news hole. This is the amount of time you need to find news stories to fill.

Here's an example for a half-hour newscast:

Goes off air at	11:28:40	Junk pages	1:00
−Goes on air at	11:00:40	Sports, weather	4:00
Newcast is	28:00	Commercials	10:00
−Extras are	15:00	Extras	15:00
News hole is	13:00		

That means you have only 13 minutes of news in your half-hour newscast. That doesn't leave you with many options for long stories.

Step Two—Make a List of Stories

A good place to start is to list the possible stories on a producer's roughsheet (see Chapter 12). Here's a list of some stories to be used in the next exercise. Call it the workbook story pool. (These stories are listed in random order.)

1. *Mayor's trip.* Mayor Bowman has returned from 10-city trip to promote Steeltown's industry. She claims to have opened new markets and has some trade agreements. You have tape now for a VO, but hope to get a package from a news conference at the airport.

2. *Out-of-town ax.* A 35-car accident on a Los Angeles freeway left two dead and tied up a major interchange for 12 hours. You have a VO.

3. *Crime spree.* Two escapees from a state prison have terrorized the northern part of the state. Their string of crimes continues with a bank robbery where one patron is shot. You have a reader.

4. *Economic predictions.* A local bank says the regional economy will prosper through the next fiscal year. Employment will be up. You have a reader.

5. *Transit mess.* Consultants agreed with what everyone knew—the local Rapid Transit Bus System is poorly managed and is facing labor problems. Right now this is a reader.

6. *City budget.* City administrators release next year's budget. It holds the line on taxes but will cut 10 percent of the police force and school budget to save money. You have a VO now, but might be able to get a videotape package on that one.

7. *Fraud trial.* The criminal trial for a former city attorney continues. He is charged with taking an aged client's money from her trust account. He invested the money for himself. You have a reader.

8. *Ambulance service.* City officials are investigating the ambulance service after complaints that the response time is very high and that the service doesn't have enough equipment in the vehicles. This story was uncovered by the local newspaper. You have a VO.

9. *Car into bank.* A motorist whose foot slipped from the brake to the accelerator made a drive-in visit to the lobby of a local bank. The car went through the front doors and ended up next to a teller's window. No one hurt. Damage was minor. You have a videotape package.

10. *State budget.* It's up 21 percent this year, mostly for higher salaries. The state hopes to get the new money by raising property taxes. You have a reader.

11. *Warehouse strike.* The 12th day of local public warehouse workers' strike. Little effect on shipping. You have a VO.

12. *Reading.* Reading scores are up for all grades at local schools. That's good news for superintendent Lyle Whippem, who advocates a back-to-basics approach. That's a reader.

13. *Recall.* The proponents of a recall drive against the school board say they have enough signatures to put it on the next ballot. You have a reader.

14. *Tickets.* City traffic officials announced they are raising the cost of a parking ticket from $20 to $30. This, they hope, will raise additional $$ for the city. You have a VO.

Step Three—Complete the Roughsheet

From the story list, divide the stories into categories on the producer's roughsheet. Identify which are must-run stories and which are minor stories. See Figure 13.1 for an example.

FIGURE 13.1
Roughsheet of day's stories.

Must-run video stories	Must-run readers
Mayor's trip—VO City budget—VO Ambulance—VO	Recall Reading Transit mess Crime spree
Minor video stories	**Minor readers**
LA ax—VO Car/bank—PKG Warehouse—VO Tickets—VO	Fraud Econ State budget

Step Four—Find the Leads

Next, select stories that are of possible lead caliber.

Must-Run Stories		Minor Stories	
Lead City budget	VO	Econ	Reader
Lead Mayor's trip	VO	Tickets	VO
Crime spree	Reader	Car/bank	PKG
Reading	Reader	LA ax	VO
Ambulance	VO	Fraud	Reader
Transit mess	Reader	State budget	Reader
Recall	Reader	Warehouse	VO

Step Five—Assign Times and Check Totals

Your subtraction has given you a news-hole running time of 13:00. Now you want to start laying out your stories on a sheet of scratch paper. Then begin to assign story lengths. If you don't reach the total of 13:00, start to plug in minor stories.

Must-Run Stories			Minor Stories		
City budget	VO	1:00	Tickets	VO	0:40
Crime spree	Read	0:40	Car/bank	PKG	2:10
Reading	Read	0:35	LA ax	VO	0:45
Ambulance	VO	1:05	Fraud	Read	0:30
Transit mess	Read	0:25	State budget	Read	0:30
Recall	Read	0:20	Warehouse	VO	1:00
Mayor's trip	VO	1:00	Econ	Read	0:25

At this point, you have only 11:05 of stories to fill 13:00. You'll probably pick up more stories, but we will expand these by adding more elements. We're going to order a package on the city budget and a package on the mayor's trip.

Step Six—Adjust Times and Sketch Out a Rundown

In this ongoing example, you'll be using an A and B segment of a commercial newscast. After you make the adjustments, you find your times are more reasonable. Give these times to the writers as story lengths.

Must-Run Stories			Minor Stories		
City budget	PKG	2:30	Tickets	VO	0:40
Crime spree	Read	0:40	Car/bank	PKG	2:10
Reading	Read	0:35	LA ax	VO	0:45
Ambulance	VO	1:05	Fraud	Read	0:30
Transit mess	Read	0:25	State budget	Read	0:30
Recall	Read	0:20	Warehouse	VO	1:00
Mayor's trip	PKG	2:30	Econ	Read	0:25

The next step is to transfer this format to the actual rundown shown in Figure 3.2.

CAST 11PM					ON AIR 11:00:40
PAGE	TAL	SLUG	VIDEO	TST	BACKTIME
A-1		CITY BUDGET	PKG	2:30	
A-2		STATE BUDGET	———	:30	
A-3		TICKETS	VO	:40	
A-4		READING	———	:35	
A-5		CRIME SPREE	———	:40	
A-6		AMBULANCE	VO	1:05	
A-7		LA AX	VO	:45	
A-8		CAR BANK	PKG	2:10	
A-9		TEASE #1	VO	:10	
		COMM #1		2:00	
B-1		MAYORS TRIP	PKG	2:30	
B-2		ECON	———	:25	
B-3		WAREHOUSE	VO	1:00	
B-4		TRANSIT MESS	———	:25	
B-5		RECALL	———	:20	
B-6		FRAUD	———	:30	
B-7		TEASE #2	VO	:10	
		COMM #2		2:00	
C-1		TOSS TO WX	———	:05	
C-2		WX	———	1:55	
		COMM #3		2:00	
D-1		TOSS TO SPORTS	———	:05	
D-2		SPORTS	———	2:00	
		COMM #4		2:00	
E-1		BYE/credits	———	:30	
		COMM #5		2:00	
NEWSCAST OFF AIR AT					11:28:40

FIGURE 13.2
Rundown for evening newscast.

You're on the way. This is a format with times and story order. It has important stories in the lead, sprinkled through the first segment, and leading the second segment. It has a softer story at the end of the first segment, although this list has no real light selections.

It also has clustering, with the city and state budget series, the mayor's trip and related economics series, the ambulance, accident, and car/bank series. It has potential for segues, and it has pacing, with no large blocks of read-only stories.

The producer did not suggest a wrap because there were no solid possibilities. Since no decisions have been made on the anchors, as yet it has no problems with pingponging.

BACKTIMING

Although computers are taking over this chore, the producer should learn to backtime a newscast. The backtime is the clock time a story should begin if the newscast is to end on time (according to the clock—not the newscast duration). It is always computed in real clock time, and is always calculated from the end of the newscast, working backward. The backtimes are important if stories must be added or dropped while the newscast is on the air.

First, it is necessary to know the exact TST (total story time) on each story. Putting the story order down on a format sheet prepares you for backtiming. If you are doing this by hand, blank format sheets should always be filled in with a pencil, to allow for scribbling when you change story TSTs and backtimes.

With a computer, these adjustments are taken care of automatically. In Figure 13.3 you can see how the subtraction scheme works. Go to the station log time for the end of the newscast, 11:28:40, and subtract the length of the Goodbye (:30) and you have the backtime for the Goodbye. To find the backtime for each story in each segment, you simply continue up the format, subtracting the story time from the backtime of the story below it. When you've got the backtime for story A-1, it should match the station log-on time at 11:00:40. In this case, it gives you a backtime showing the newscast is still :15 heavy.

Notice that two prospective stories have been removed from the newscast, in our example, the Transit and Recall stories. (Compare Figures 13.2 and 13.3.)

PAGE	TAL	SLUG	VIDEO	TST	BACKTIME

Header top: CAST 11PM — ON AIR 11:00:40

PAGE	TAL	SLUG	VIDEO	TST	BACKTIME
A-1		CITY BUDGET	PKG	2:30	11:00:25
A-2		STATE BUDGET	————	:30	11:02:55
A-3		TICKETS	VO	:40	11:03:25
A-4		READING	————	:35	11:04:05
A-5		CRIME SPREE	————	:40	11:04:40
A-6		AMBULANCE	VO	1:05	11:05:20
A-7		LA AX	VO	:45	11:06:25
A-8		CAR BANK	PKG	2:10	11:07:10
A-9		TEASE #1	VO	:10	11:09:20
		COMM #1		2:00	11:09:30
B-1		MAYORS TRIP	PKG	2:30	11:11:30
B-2		ECON	————	:25	11:14:00
B-3		WAREHOUSE	VO	1:00	11:14:25
B-6		FRAUD	————	:30	11:15:25
B-7		TEASE #2	VO	:10	11:15:55
		COMM #2		2:00	11:16:05
C-1		TOSS TO WX	————	:05	11:18:05
C-2		WX	————	2:00	11:18:10
		COMM #3		2:00	11:20:05
D-1		TOSS TO SPORTS	————	:05	11:22:05
D-2		SPORTS	————	2:00	11:22:10
		COMM #4		2:00	11:24:10
E-1		BYE/credits	————	:30	11:26:10
		COMM #5		2:00 C	11:26:40 B

NEWSCAST OFF AIR AT 11:28:40 A

To backtime, you substract the story time C
from the backtime of the story below A
and the result is your story backtime B

FIGURE 13.3
Format with backtimes.

ON-AIR DECISIONS DURING THE NEWSCAST

The producer is usually responsible for the length of the newscast, and must pull and alter stories while the program is on the air. Only the producer can make editorial changes in the booth during the newscast. Although the director must make some immediate decisions if technical needs change, the director must defer to the producer in questions of content of the newscast.

CHAPTER SUMMARY

Both the copyeditor and the producer must check all copy for accuracy, fairness, scope, libel, and writing style. The producer is responsible for planning stories, developing stories, coaching and copyediting the writers, assigning times for the reports, scheduling these in newscasts, checking to see that all stories are done, and seeing that the newscast is backtimed and produced on the air.

Index

Tuchman, Gaye, 29
TRT, 19
Upcut, 152
Uppercase fonts, 20

Verbs,
   Complexity, 48
   Effective use, 58–61
   Negative, 40–41
VO, 19, 151, 153–166, 172
VO/SOT, 151, 167–172
Voicer, 117, 127, 128, 129–131

Wire capture, 1
Wrap, 118, 127, 128, 134–137, 202
Writeup, 99, 104, 109–113